Longevity
in Leadership

Longevity
in Leadership

ESSENTIAL QUALITIES of LONGTIME LEADERS

PHILLIP V. LEWIS

JOHN P. HARRISON

Abilene Christian University Press

LONGEVITY IN LEADERSHIP
Essential Qualities of Longtime Leaders

ACU
PRESS

Copyright © 2016 by Phillip V. Lewis and John P. Harrison

ISBN 978-0-89112-665-2

Printed in the United States of America

Cover design by Jeannette Munger
Interior text design by Sandy Armstrong

For information contact:
Abilene Christian University Press
ACU Box 29138
Abilene, Texas 79699

1-877-816-4455
www.acupressbooks.com

16 17 18 19 20 21 22 / 7 6 5 4 3 2 1

Marilyn H. Lewis
Sharon F. Harrison
Leaders in their own right

Table of Contents

Go the Distance: Endeavor

Foreword

Thersippus. Not a household name. But what Thersippus accomplished is celebrated in cities and towns around the world every year as a symbol of human determination, endurance, and fortitude.

Why Thersippus's name is not familiar to most people is an interesting story. Robert Browning, the great English poet, wrote a poem in 1879 named "Pheidippides." In it, he alludes to a story first told by a satirist named Lucian in the second century AD. Lucian claimed that a soldier named Pheidippides was sent from the Greek town of Marathon to tell the Athenian elders that the Greek army had defeated the Persians in the battle of Marathon (in 490 BC), saving the city from its enemies. As this story is repeated in Browning's poem, Pheidippides arrives before the elders after his approximately twenty-five-mile nonstop run and exclaims, "Rejoice! We conquered!" and then immediately dies. Browning's poem of this dedicated long-distance runner so inspired Baron Pierre de Coubertin and others that they created a race for the Olympics and named it a *marathon*.

But Pheidippides wasn't the one who ran nonstop from Marathon to Athens! It was a herald named Thersippus. While most people may never know to give credit to Thersippus, his remarkable physical strength is nevertheless remembered when men and women lace up their shoes, brave all types of weather conditions, and push their bodies and minds to produce the resilience needed to complete a marathon. There is something admirable about people who demonstrate the ability to overcome momentary pain and obstacles to go the distance and achieve a goal that most are not willing to sacrifice in order to achieve.

The same thing can be said of leaders who go the distance and serve for a long time. Everybody knows that leading is challenging. Leaders are out front showing people and organizations new places where they can and should go. They have to inspire people to challenge themselves to do more things or to increase their abilities in order to achieve specific goals. Often this is not easy. Real success hardly ever is. The road is difficult and treacherous. Rebellion and failure are not uncommon. People can be resistant to demands and expectations placed upon them by those who are leading them. Leaders have to learn to be diplomatic yet decisive. They have to be encouraging while insisting on momentum. They have to be a reassuring voice while also requiring discipline.

These are but a few of the things a leader must do in order to go the distance. The whole gamut of activities required of leaders includes tasks that are not easy to perform and not easy to keep in balance. If leaders are so focused on achieving goals that they fail to build cohesion, then they will be perceived as tyrants, autocrats, or organizational bullies. If they capitulate to every whim and cry of those they are trying to lead in order to keep people happy, then they are unlikely to reach the outcome they were charged to produce. No, leaders—successful leaders, that is— push through the pain, hurdle the obstacles, and press ahead to the goals, bringing along to the finish line the ones who trust them.

We frequently work with and alongside leaders in business and in churches and have written this book with those who currently are leading or want to lead in mind. We know that leading often can be discouraging work, and we want to encourage both leaders and potential leaders to stay the course and lead effectively and successfully for a long time. Our hope is that the life-learned lessons that have been shared with us by longtime leaders will guide and motivate you to become a leader who will go the distance.

Completing this book has required a lot of patience, determination, and endurance. We know that the weight of our work has been made lighter because of the encouragement from our wives and their sacrifices of time with us to give us the time this project has required. For their partnership in life and for cheering us on to the finish, we are sincerely and deeply grateful. You have blessed our lives.

CHAPTER 1

Design a Long-Distance Career

As I urged you when I went into Macedonia, stay there in Ephesus so that you may commend certain people not to teach false doctrines any longer or to devote themselves to myths and endless genealogies. Such things promote controversial speculations rather than advancing God's work—which is by faith.

1 Timothy 1:3–4

Have you ever wondered why certain individuals are productive in their career yet they do not advance? Or how some hang on to a job seemingly forever without continuing to be very productive? On the other hand, some people stay in a career for many years and advance while continuing to be productive. For example, Brett Favre is one of the few quarterbacks in NFL history to play for more than twenty years. He threw more than 10,000 passes for over 70,000 yards, 500 touchdowns, and 300 interceptions. He retired in January 2011 after playing for four different teams. Other quarterbacks are drafted, play a little, and disappear in just a few short years. What makes the difference? How do some people have such sustained energy and effort? What is the key to endurance? Can longevity be cultivated?

In corporate America the average life expectancy of a Fortune 500 company is estimated to be about forty years. Yet the career lives of those promoted to senior vice president, executive vice president, or chief executive officer are estimated at only two years in one position or company. John McKee, a leadership coach writing about the corporate world, says, "Today, if your life has a letter in front of it—like S [Senior], E [Executive], or C [Chief]—be prepared to have the lifespan of an earthworm."[1]

What explains the lack of longevity in senior leadership roles? Perhaps the executive suite is not as glamorous as people imagine it to be.

The outlook doesn't look much better for professional ministers. The average time of service in a church is about four years. Apparently, too many ministers leave in that third or fourth year, when other church leaders begin to test their likelihood of becoming a real leader in the church. Sensing this pushback from church leaders, many ministers interpret such resistance as a danger sign and start looking for another job. This turnover, however, can have truly damaging effects on churches. George Barna, founder of the Barna Group, a research firm specializing in Christian organizations, has found that "pastors experience their most productive and influential ministry in years five through fourteen of their pastorate."[2] If ministers are leaving before their fifth year, they never stay long enough to become effective, according to Barna's research.

There are many theories about longevity and many sources of purported "secrets," such as the one on the front cover of the June 2012 issue of Southwest Airlines *Spirit* magazine. In small print at the bottom of the page was the following: "The secret to longevity? A little bit of old-time rock 'n' roll." The *Spirit* cover reminds us that nearly everyone is interested in the subject of longevity—durability, endurance, or long life.

The Bible includes many interesting statements on the subject. For example, the apostle Paul wrote: "Children, obey your parents in the Lord, for this is right. 'Honor your father and mother'—which is the first commandment with a promise—'so that it may go well with you and that you may enjoy long life on the earth'" (Eph. 6:1–3). In Proverbs, the sage likewise admonishes his pupil to "not forget my teaching, but keep my commands in your heart, for they will prolong your life many years and bring you peace and prosperity" (3:1–2). This commandment, when fully understood, is directed not only to youth, but also to all who are children of God. When we obey our heavenly Father, our lives are blessed. As King David wrote, "I was young and now I am old, yet I have never seen the righteous forsaken or their children begging bread" (Ps. 37:25).

In the verse that opens this chapter, the apostle Paul tells Timothy to stay in Ephesus because he knew the times were difficult and those early Christians needed more time to mature and become comfortable in the new faith in Jesus to which they had committed themselves. Timothy might have preferred to go on with Paul, but false teachers were already attempting to distort what Paul had taught. Paul knew the Ephesians needed to learn more from Timothy so they would not be deceived into corrupting their faith under the pretense that the false teachers could improve it. They would need coaching to embrace the gospel as it was delivered to them.

Leadership then and now can be difficult. But jumping ship when the waves seem turbulent won't stop the storm, and it won't save the ship—in fact, it might leave the ship more vulnerable. The late James K. Bridges, a former general treasurer for the Assemblies of God, wrote, "Rapid pastoral turnover greatly contributes to the instability, lack of growth, and the demise of a local church."[3]

Another One Bites the Dust

In reviewing leadership transitions from the news cycle in 2010, John McKee noted that prominent executives faced dismissal for three key reasons:

1. *Performance issues.* At Apple, senior vice president Mark Papermaster lost the confidence of the late Steve Jobs after about a year because Jobs had not seen increased productivity and profits. The problems occurred even though Jobs had personally hired this twenty-year IBM veteran with an impressive track record.

2. *Lifestyle issues.* Hewlett Packard fired CEO Mark Hurd for indiscretions, such as falsifying expense reports, a not-so-smart romantic relationship with a former movie actress, and a less-than-forthcoming response when questioned about those issues.

3. *Poor people skills.* CEO Tony Hayward of British Petroleum was fired because of the impact of the Gulf oil disaster, his arrogance, and an indication of little resolve to fix things quickly.[4]

You would think, as much publicity as problems like these have received in the last couple of decades, that everyone would have their antennas up to make sure they don't fall into a similar trap. Yet every year leaders involve themselves in this type of untoward activities. Are they really that dense? What's missing in our personal and professional development?

In his Gospel, Luke says, "Jesus grew in wisdom and in stature, and in favor with God and man" (2:52). This verse is often said to mean that Jesus grew in his mental, physical, spiritual, and social development. Bridges suggests that professionals should look to excel in these same four areas over a long-term career.

1. *Mental stability.* We must strive to keep our mental attitude in alignment with the word of God in order to have healthy and biblical thought processes. What we think, we do; and what we do, we become. It is essential that we strive to stay mentally refreshed, alert, and logical. Everyone needs a close friend with whom to test thinking.

2. *Physical stability.* We must look to the Lord for our health. We must use discipline, restraint, and wisdom to stay in the best possible physical shape.

3. *Spiritual stability.* Staying spiritually healthy is vital to our tenure. We must be known as people of spiritual moderation. That means we are people of prayer, of the word, and of the Spirit, whose walk with Christ is close and personal, showing spiritual maturity.

4. *Social stability*. Having a proper relationship with people requires that we have emotional maturity. Emotional instability may manifest itself in many ways, such as an explosive temperament or an inferiority complex. Jesus modeled a relationship with people that came from having the wisdom of God. James describes such wisdom as "from above." He says it is "pure, peaceable, gentle, willing to yield, full of mercy and good fruits, without partiality, and without hypocrisy" (3:17).[5]

Christian author and speaker John Maxwell writes, "A leader must exemplify competence, connection, and character."[6] A leader with character is one who faithfully develops competence, character, and connection over a long period of time.

The Qualities of Longevity

Longevity is signified by staying power. Joleen Spencer, formerly a senior vice president of marketing with Shore Bank, in a 2009 interview defined staying power as "the ability to stand in good times and bad times coupled with the ability to be gracious in victory and resilient in defeat."[7] However, you will not be promoted simply for demonstrating you can occupy a seat at a desk and repeat tasks; that is, you need to demonstrate maturity, not just longevity. You will be expected to be accountable for fulfilling your job description.

Roberta Shaler explains, "Accountability requires that you take the initiative to learn your tasks. Ask questions. Read books. Keep up with your industry by reading newsletters and trade journals. Request training and use it well. Knowing your job reduces your stress. Exceeding your job's expectations leads to promotion."[8]

According to Charmon Parker Williams, principal consultant and president of Parker Williams Consulting, "The ability to enhance career longevity is enhanced by defining your value proposition (i.e., your worth), proactively building solid relationships, and having a sense of purpose and principles."[9] But exactly what are the actual qualities that will contribute to a leader's longevity?

Anecdotal Evidence

If you are not the founder and CEO of a company or if you did not inherit the enterprise from your parents, how will you beat the impossible odds against having staying power? If you are the primary minister of a church, how will you develop staying power? Some leaders base their understanding of longevity on mere anecdotal evidence. Usually wrapped in warm personal stories, the anecdotes are anchored little nuggets of wisdom. Perhaps, you have heard them before:

- Reproduce yourself
- Be willing to learn
- Hang in there
- Buckle your seat belt; it's going to be a bumpy ride"

These truisms—and the stories that surround them—are well intentioned, but they are not based on actual research into how to sustain oneself as a longtime leader. The actual characteristics common to longevity include innovation, resiliency, focus, and adaptability. Traits and skills include integrity, personality characteristics, personal interactions, technical capability, intuition, and professional knowledge. People who make a positive difference are said to be competent, consistent, credible, and courageous.

Primary Research

Based on the need for trustworthy data (instead of anecdotal information), the authors interviewed and sent a questionnaire to several ministers and business leadership experts, both male and female, who had developed long, productive careers at their churches or organizations. We asked what they would consider to be the top ten qualities of a person who has enjoyed long-term success. How does one build a prolonged career? We asked them. Their responses yielded almost one hundred forty distinct and yet related items.

When we conducted this primary research, we used self-reported surveys, a common technique in the field of psychology referred to as "social perception." This technique attempts to discover participants' inner thoughts by having respondents report their perceptions, with the assumption that the respondents' descriptions are indicative of their inner feelings. The validity of such research is enhanced when the respondents are allowed to answer in free-form as opposed to being constrained by a set of prescribed dimensions.

After the responses were collected, analysis by the authors proceeded in three stages: First, each response was examined to identify those concepts expressed. Second, the concepts were grouped into a smaller number of identified qualities of longevity. Third, the authors' groupings were compared, and agreement was reached on four categories with three characteristics of longevity in each, for a total of twelve traits essential to longevity.

We believe the four qualities of longevity are best represented by the acronym **TEAM**—*Trust, Endeavor, Aim,* and *Motivate.* These qualities will be discussed in more depth in Chapters Two through Thirteen, but an overview of the TEAM concept is provided here.

Trust

Longevity insists on trust. The three qualities we identified under trust are trust in God, trust in others, and trust in self. Leaders with staying power create and benefit from an environment of trust, which increases confidence, reliance, expectation, and hope. Leaders who place trust in others and themselves believe in the honesty, truthfulness, justice, or power of God and others. They seek constancy, congruity, and reliability, and work to win the respect of others, develop mutual feelings of trust, and establish open lines of communication. Such leaders create climates conducive to spiritual productivity. Healthy trusting relationships encourage people to achieve their full potential.

Trust takes time, which is why leadership longevity is crucial. Trust requires a substance of character that consistently does the right thing, depends on leadership transparency and authenticity, and happens in relational contexts of healthy, loving interaction. Trust is hard to gain and easy to lose. Thus, the idea of cultivating trust must be kept on the front burners of your life and leadership.

Endeavor

Longevity requires an endeavor, which is exerting oneself in order to affect change. Endeavoring might be thought of as going the second mile, bending over backwards, giving it your best shot, or going all out. For example, a particular church could be endeavoring to help orphans in developing countries, or another church might be endeavoring to expand its missions outreach.

You may recall that after the 1986 loss of the Challenger space shuttle, the United States built the space shuttle *Endeavour,* which was named after the British sea Captain James Cook's eighteenth-century ship of discovery (hence the British spelling of "endeavor"). Its first flight in May 1992 may best be remembered for its service mission to the Hubble Space Telescope. Just as the *Endeavour* took its crew into new experiences, long-term leaders have a history of taking their organizations or churches to new places, new experiences, and new levels of understanding.

In addition to using the word *endeavor*, we often use the word *endure*. The word *endure* can often be seen to have a negative meaning, such as "to tolerate," "to put up with," or "to bear with." However, we are using *endure* in a more positive sense, such as when the apostle Paul used "endure" to convey a positive attitude toward suffering and afflictions as experiences through which God works in the world. He does this when he encourages Timothy to endure (2 Tim. 2:3 KJV) or when he admonishes the Romans to be patient in suffering as a means of letting love be sincere (12:12).

Within this positive sense of *endure*, we recognize three characteristics under the category of endeavor: high levels of energy, the ability to handle criticism, and the sense of working for a cause bigger than self. Businesses and churches need dedicated people who will stay the course, who can teach, train, model, and lead. On occasion, we may be serving in a difficult place or in a different culture. Sometimes our leadership is met with opposition and resistance. We must positively endure until we have completed whatever God has appointed us to do. One minister put it this way, "Ministers must endure the ministry, ministry must endure the trials, and ministry must be continued until it's complete."[10]

To endeavor requires the energy to run a long distance. Success is the result of a healthy mindset, preparation, practice, and staying focused on what lies ahead. Victory doesn't depend on how you start. It requires your willingness to practice and maintain a positive attitude in order to build up endurance. It depends on your support system and the ability to withstand the naysayers. A leader with staying power will respond pleasantly, positively, and professionally to the critic. He or she may carry a spiritual shield but not a spiritual machete.

Finally, long-term leaders work for a cause worthy of their life. As Norman Vincent Peale, former New York City minister and author, once said: "The more you lose yourself in something bigger than yourself, the more energy you will have."[11]

Aim

Longevity requires an aim—an aspiration for endeavor. The three qualities we identify under *aim* are keeping the main thing the main thing, seeing what people can become, and developing an inner circle of support. Aim suggests the need for a vision of what you want your organization to be—a dream. Some people confuse vision statements with mission statements, but until you have identified the dream and know what it is, you can't develop a strategy to get you there or the tactics to meet the strategy—that is, you can't create or sustain the main thing. It is imperative that everyone in the organization understands the need to keep the main thing the main thing and buys into it with passion.

Seeing what people can become implies an understanding of personal development. In some cases, seeing what someone might become requires a willingness to mentor that person, share advice, and develop a relationship. For example, you may have specific experience and expertise in the same field as a person in whom you see something special, and you know this person needs your assistance. Your aim is to contribute to their successful performance on the job.

Motivate

Achieving longevity requires developing the ability to motivate others. The three characteristics we identify under the category of *motivate* are developing others, keeping good lines of communication open, and being a good listener. A number of motivational theories have been proposed and corollaries applied in social behavior theory. However, there seem to be two basic ways to look at motivation. The traditional view defines motivation as *a process of directing people to action in order to accomplish a desired goal.* Accordingly, leaders motivate followers and are self-motivated to achieve goals and objectives. A more current view describes motivation as *the creation of a state of tension and disequilibrium that causes the individual to move in a goal-directed pattern toward need satisfaction and equilibrium.* Both center on goal achievement, whether it is internally or externally driven. Intrinsic motivation arises from performance of tasks; extrinsic motivation is external and results from rewards, incentives, or promotions.

Motivation affects everything we do. It is the sum of all our intrinsic and extrinsic motivations. It determines the way Christians serve God—halfheartedly out of obligation or zealously out of gratefulness for his saving grace. Successful leaders are motivators who keep an open-door policy and open lines of communication; they share information transparently and listen with intent to understand. The fact that they are optimistic, positive, affirming, cheerful, and willing to praise others in their messages contributes powerfully to their career longevity and the admiration of their followers.

The Long Haul

Based on the TEAM acronym, where do you stand on developing or sustaining the qualities of longevity: trust, endeavor, aim, and motivate? Do you feel sometimes like you're just paying your dues? Are you staying ahead of the curve and remaining competitive? Or are you falling behind? In a 2009 interview, William McKnight Farrow, III, who was then the CIO for the Chicago Board of Trade, said, "Staying current is not the challenge. Staying invigorated and enthusiastic is."[12]

We know that success doesn't just happen overnight; it doesn't just suddenly emerge. It takes a lot of hard work, sometimes atrocious hours, occasional failure, and personal and family sacrifices. One has to balance value with commitment.

We've all been taught to eat our grains, vegetables, and fruit. We've been cautioned about the dangers of alcohol and tobacco. We have agreed to abide by the laws about seatbelts and speed. We've learned how to help extend our lives by adopting healthy and safe habits. Now it's time we learn something about how to extend our careers.

Follow the TEAM formula! Trust. Endeavor. Aim. Motivate.

Reality Check (Q/A)

1. Think of someone who has demonstrated sustained energy and effort on the job. What has been the key to their endurance? How did they cultivate longevity?

2. Think of short-time executives or ministers who seemed to leave their organization before their time. Why do you think they were unable to discover the secret of longevity?

3. Why do you think obeying your parents—honoring your father and mother—results in the enjoyment of long life?

4. Why should leaders who have an S, E, or C in front of their job title expect to have the lifespan of an earthworm?

5. If you were to pick one of the four spiritual areas in which to excel in order to have a long-term career, which one would it be? Why? Discuss.

6. If you had to name the most important qualities that contribute to a leader's longevity, which qualities would be on your list? Why?

7. Would you agree that trust requires evidence of a substance in character that leads a person to consistently do the right thing? Why?

8. Why do you think success is the result of a healthy mindset, preparation, practice, and staying focused on what lies ahead?

9. How does your aim contribute to successful performance on the job? Discuss.

10. Do you agree or disagree that leaders with staying power view motivation as being related to activities both in and out of the organization? Why?

11. Based on the TEAM acronym, where do you stand on developing or sustaining the qualities of longevity? Discuss.

12. If someone who has not studied longevity asked you how to extend his or her career, how would you answer? Discuss.

Case Study: Longevity[13]

The Concho Rio Church has a family minister, Lucas Rodriguez, age 46, who specializes in family and church development based on the belief that churches can't be built up and grown without strong families. Rodriquez has been at Concho Rio since 2003. His long-range goal is to build a durable career that will withstand severe hardships as well as times of smooth sailing. He believes that if he stands tough as nails, he will have a huge advantage for longevity during the second half of his life and career.

Concerning his ministry, he says, "I wasn't satisfied with the products available on the market. We needed a new direction in family emphasis. I wanted a product that I could stand behind. I wanted to make our corner of the world better than it ever was by encouraging strong families and developing a church that would attract newcomers."

The results have been successful. The training workshops implemented by Rodriguez have gone well, and the attendee responses have been quite satisfactory. The church has grown at about a two percent rate per year during the past decade.

After ten years, however, Rodriguez is beginning to question whether his dream of a long career is critical to the church. Fortunately, he has full support of the senior minister and church leaders. He is beginning to question himself as to what can be done to extend the life and success of his career and programs. What is missing from his life, church relationships, ministerial camaraderie, continuing education, or other areas that would affect his perspective on how durability and longevity affect his church service function?

He recently signed up to attend a two-day workshop on longevity in Dallas that looks promising on paper. Rodriguez is excited about the possibilities and what the workshop might mean for the remaining years of his church career.

1. If you were the instructor at the longevity workshop, what would your workshop outline look like?
2. How would you address maturity versus longevity at the workshop?
3. If you asked a half-dozen people at your workplace or church what they think the qualities of longevity are, what do you think their responses would be?

Notes

[1] John McKee, "The Executive Suite Is Not So Sweet," *Tech Decision Maker* (Blog), *Tech Republic / U.S.*, August 11, 2010, http://www.techrepublic.com/blog/tech-decision-maker/the-executive-suite-is-not-so-sweet/.

[2] George Barna, *The Second Coming of the Church* (Nashville: Thomas Nelson, 1998), 5.

[3] James K. Bridges, "Pastoral Longevity," *Enrichment Journal*, Winter 2001, http://enrichmentjournal.ag.org/200101/0101_106_longevity.cfm/.

[4] McKee, "Executive Suite."

[5] Bridges, "Pastoral Longevity."

[6] John C. Maxwell, *Ultimate Leadership: Maximize Your Potential and Empower Your Team* (Nashville: Thomas Nelson, 2007), 68.

[7] Charmon Parker Williams, "Staying Power: Techniques for Longevity," *Diversity MBA Magazine*, December 21, 2009, http://diversitymbamagazine.com/staying-power-techniques-for-longevity/.

[8] Roberta Shaler, "Maturity or Just Longevity?," *Career-Intelligence.com,* Accessed July 11, 2015., http://www.career-intelligence.com/management/Longevity.asp.

[9] Charmon Parker Williams, "Staying Power: Techniques for Longevity."

[10] Bridges, "Pastoral Longevity."

[11] Norman Vincent Peale, *The Power of Positive Thinking: 10 Traits for Maximum Results*, reprint edition, (New York: Simon & Schuster, 2003), 35.

[12] Williams, "Staying Power."

[13] All case studies presented in this book are hypothetical; any resemblance to real persons, companies, churches, or situations is coincidental.

GO THE DISTANCE:
TRUST

TRUST GOD

TRUST OTHERS

TRUST SELF

CHAPTER 2

Trust God

The Lord is my strength and my shield;
my heart trusts in him, and he helps me.

Psalm 28:7

In a *New Yorker* article titled "In God They Trust: Washington faces a new challenge: Should it let the churches take over the inner cities?" columnist Joe Klein tells the story of Joy of Jesus, an urban mission organization in the city of Detroit.[1] The goal of this community organization was to provide a job-training program for welfare recipients, some who faced enormous financial challenges.

As a part of the program, all participants were led in prayer and in Bible study. Participation in Joy for Jesus increased so much, and it successfully prepared so many of the unemployed to get jobs that then-governor of Michigan, John Engler, thought it should be funded with the aid of other secular agencies. However, in exchange for these additional funds, Joy for Jesus would have to stop leading participants in prayer and Bible study. At first, the organization agreed to these requirements, but after nearly a year under these restrictions, its rate of successfully placing the unemployed into jobs *dropped* even though it was now better-funded. So Joy for Jesus decided to return the money and returned to prayer and Bible study along with job training.

The organization's leaders came to realize that the program could not thrive when they were not doing what they believed God wanted them to do. Their decision came down to a matter of trust. Were they going to trust God with their ministry and do what they believed would please him, or would they trust that the extra funds would make them more successful? In the end, they chose to trust what they knew would please God.

The Joy for Jesus experience illustrates one of the most fundamental lessons for every Christian leader: trusting God matters. Nearly every book on leadership will at some point raise the issue of trust. Leadership either succeeds with it or fails without it. Not every author stresses the importance of trusting God, but in our discussions with longtime leaders, we have learned that trusting God made the crucial difference in their leadership tenure.

What Does It Mean to "Trust God"?

All Christians know that "trust" or "faith" in God and in Jesus is central to their relationship with God. It's like the ballast on two sides of a ship. On the night that he was betrayed, Jesus told his disciples, "Trust in God; trust also in me" (John 14:1 NLT). Jesus tied the relationship he would have with his followers to their trust in God. To trust one is to trust the other. Without trusting in Jesus, they could not have the relationship with God that they desired.

Paul also urged Titus to insist that the Christians on Crete trust in God and devote themselves to good works (Tit. 3:8). Paul knew that the foundation of a Christian's experience with God, as well as with each other, is grounded in trust.

Trusting in God essentially entails accepting his will for our lives as our authority and obeying that will to the best of our ability, especially in the face of circumstances that tempt us to trust ourselves and our own judgments. The more we trust in our own power, intellect, reason, or emotion rather than in God's authority, the less we are trusting God.

An old Puritan dictum states, "Suspect thyself much."[2] We will never be able to trust God too much, but we often trust ourselves too completely. When leaders trust God, they will do what they believe God wants them to do even when competing actions seem to be more beneficial or rational.

Why Should Leaders Trust God?

This question is a lot more complicated than it would first appear. Someone might simply claim that leaders must trust God because God requires it. This argument is certainly true. In both the Old and New Testaments leaders are admonished to trust God as they face huge obstacles that would tempt them to do otherwise. But trusting God does not come with some kind of Pollyanna promise that leaders who trust will always get what they want. It is abundantly self-evident that many leaders who have put their trust in God do not see their hopes and dreams of a long-term leadership materialize. Lots of leaders have trusted God only to later be shown the exit door.

Trusting God is not a failsafe action which will guarantee that leaders will never face trials or adversity. For example, the leadership at Chick-fil-A learned about adversity when it took a stand against gay marriage and had to listen to unfounded allegations against them by advocate organizations and by some politicians and newspapers. Although the organization seems to have weathered the storm, the controversy proves that simply trusting God will not stop the rain.

So, if trusting God doesn't automatically insure a leader's success, why do so many Christian leaders say their trust of God has contributed to their longevity as a leader? How does trusting God enable leaders and change them so that they can lead for a long time? In order to answer this question, it would be helpful to look at biblical leaders who did trust God. What does their trust reveal about their character?

Biblical Leaders Who Trusted God

Numerous stories in Scripture showcase leaders who trusted God. These events demonstrate the tremendous difference this trust made in their lives. Several lessons about trust could be gleaned from the actions taken by these men and women in Scripture. We could examine the story of Joseph, who trusted God even when he was falsely accused of attacking Potiphar's wife. Or we could turn to the example of Moses, who trusted God and confronted Pharaoh even though he was not eloquent and he didn't have an army. Just as easily, we could look at King David. Although he had faults and failures, he nevertheless directed his heart toward God and led for a long time. Then there is the example of Queen Esther, who chose to risk her own life to do what would protect God's people.

The list of great biblical leaders could go on and on. But two stories that showcase longtime leaders who trusted God are often overlooked even though they contain important insight into why trusting God is characteristic of longevity in leadership.

King Hezekiah Trusts God

The author of 2 Chronicles tells the story of King Hezekiah's leadership over Judah. Hezekiah became king when he was twenty-five years old. In order to appreciate the extent to which Hezekiah trusted God, recall the faithlessness during the reign of his father, King Ahaz, a leader who clearly did not trust Israel's God. Because the gods of the Assyrians seemed to help the Assyrians become powerful, Ahaz decided to trust them. Israel's God, Yahweh, seemed to do nothing for Ahaz, so the king decided only to trust those gods he believed could make him powerful and exalted. Ahaz turned his back on Yahweh, built places to sacrifice to the Assyrian gods, and destroyed the utensils that were used in the Temple to worship the Lord (2 Chron. 28:22–25).

Despite his attempts to exalt himself, Ahaz's reign ended in shame. Although he was given a burial in Jerusalem, the people did not bury him with their other kings. In death, Ahaz did not receive the exaltation he so desperately craved. He turned his back on God, and in the end the people he reigned over turned their backs on him.

Then along came twenty-five-year-old Hezekiah. The chronicler tells readers that this young king "did what was right in the sight of the LORD" (2 Chron. 29:2). In other words, Hezekiah turned his back on his father's idolatrous practices and instead sought to repair the damage his father had done to the Temple. He cleansed it of defilements, restored proper worship there, reorganized the duties of priests and Levites, held the Passover festival according to the rules of purity, and destroyed the pagan shrines in several places (2 Chron. 29–31). He did what he believed would honor God among the people.

However, of all the great deeds that Hezekiah accomplished, one of the greatest tests of whether or not he was going to trust God is described in 2 Chronicles 32:1–8.

After all that Hezekiah had so faithfully done, Sennacherib king of Assyria came and invaded Judah. He laid siege to the fortified cities, thinking to conquer them for himself. When Hezekiah saw that Sennacherib had come and that he intended to wage war against Jerusalem, he consulted with his officials and military staff about blocking off the water from the springs outside the city, and they helped him. They gathered a large group of people who blocked all the springs and the stream that flowed through the land. "Why should the kings of Assyria come and find plenty of water?" they said. Then he worked hard repairing all the broken sections of the wall and building towers on it. He built another wall outside that one and reinforced the terraces of the City of David. He also made large numbers of weapons and shields.

He appointed military officers over the people and assembled them before him in the square at the city gate and encouraged them with these words: "Be strong and courageous. Do not be afraid or discouraged because of the king of Assyria and the vast army with him, for there is a greater power with us than with him. With him is only the arm of flesh, but with us is the Lord our God to help us and to fight our battles." And the people gained confidence from what Hezekiah the king of Judah said.

Hezekiah faced a massive military threat. The most reasonable and beneficial thing for him to do would be to make peace with Sennacherib, then serve him and his gods. But Hezekiah did the harder thing. He trusted God to deliver the people from the Assyrian army. And God answered Hezekiah's trust and prayers. Sennacherib's army was defeated, and Sennacherib's own sons later rose up and killed him.

Like Hezekiah, leaders who will last for a long time will face obstacles and adversities—some that are more powerful than they are. But instead of choosing to live in fear and do things that dishonor God (lie, cheat, meet our enemies' evil with evil), Christian leaders trust God and continue to take actions that they know will honor him (speak the truth, deal justly, render kindness for evil). They know the one they serve is greater and will fight their true enemy.

Apostles Peter and John Trust God

Most readers of the Gospels and the book of Acts are familiar with the apostles Peter and John. They are remembered in the Gospels as some of the first followers of Jesus, along with their brothers Andrew and James. Neither of them was a perfect follower by any means. Peter is often depicted as the one who speaks up before anyone else and is willing to act boldly, if sometimes too impetuously. But Peter is also remembered as the one who made the great confession that Jesus is the Messiah, the Son of the living God, and was promised that upon "this rock" (Peter and his confession) Jesus would build his church (Matt. 16:16–19).

John and his brother James impertinently asked to have seats of authority on Jesus' right and left after he came into his kingdom (Mark 10:37). But Jesus thought so much of John, James, and Peter that he took them up on the mountain where he was transfigured and confirmed to be God's Son (Mark 9:2–8); and on the night before he was to be executed, he wanted these three men nearby (Mark 14:33). Jesus undoubtedly saw in them the potential to be great leaders of his disciples.

Peter and John did become leaders in the early church. On the day of Pentecost, it was Peter who spoke to the crowd and charged them with crucifying God's Messiah (Acts 2:36). It was Peter and John who went to confirm the conversion of Samaritans (Acts 8:14–17). Peter was the first person to convert a Gentile (Acts 10). Later he died for his allegiance to Christ. James was one of the early Christian martyrs (Acts 12:2). John, according to church tradition, served Jesus and led followers, especially through his letters and Gospel, until his death as an old man. But among the several descriptions of their lives as leaders in Christ's church, one instance in Acts 4 well illustrates the trust that Peter and John held in God.

The movement of Jesus followers was growing in Jerusalem daily (Acts 2:47). On one occasion, as Peter and John were going to the Temple to pray, they came across a crippled beggar whom they healed in Jesus' name. The healed man was so thankful that he clung to Peter and John, and a crowd ran to see what had happened. Peter looked at the crowd and saw another opportunity to preach about Jesus. Again he accused the crowd of participating in Jesus' execution (Acts 3:15). But he also told them that God had raised Jesus from the dead and was now willing to forgive them of their sins if they would repent (Acts 3:19).

The Temple authorities became aware of what Peter and John were preaching and feared that their preaching could cause the crowd to rebel against their authority. This could have caused an uproar, something the Romans would have frowned upon and crushed immediately. So the Jerusalem rulers, including the high priests, arrested Peter and John and instructed them not to preach anymore in the name of Jesus.

It is at that moment when Peter and John's strong leadership qualities shone brightly. There, in front of the Jewish council that had the authority to scourge them, Peter and John showed that they would trust God. Instead of trying to save their own lives, they told council members, "Which is right in God's eyes: to listen to you, or to him? You be the judges! As for us, we cannot help speaking about what we have seen and heard" (Acts 4:19–20).

Trusting God looks like this: leaders who trust God do not compromise on their convictions about what God wants them to do. When situations arise and they are tempted to do something other than what God would have them do, they stand by their faith in God and are willing to suffer any repercussions. Trusting God is more valuable than saving one's reputation, one's position, even one's life. Peter and John trusted God, and that trust contributed to their formation as leaders who could last.

How Does Trusting God Affect Long-Term Leadership?

Every leader has two huge questions they must answer. They must first ask themselves, "Who am I?" Then they must ask, "Who are the people I lead?" How leaders answer these two questions will determine their ability to lead. Leaders with an unhealthy perception of either who they truly are or who they are truly leading often will become disastrous leaders. Some leaders worship themselves; they end up becoming their own god. Worship of self is an easy step to take. It is taken all the time. Sometimes it is taken boldly, as when a leader says privately, "I don't trust anybody but myself!" Other times it is more camouflaged, as when leaders believe that their self-worth depends on how successful they become. But whether bold or hidden, a leader who worships self is not trusting in God. It means putting oneself in the place where God should be. God calls this idolatry.

Leaders who see themselves as the only person they can trust (even though they have a circle of followers) invariably look upon those they lead primarily as people who exist to elevate them. When leaders value the people they lead only for how much honor they bring to their leaders, unhealthy practices ensue. These egocentric leaders take advantage of other people's trust and end up manipulating others.

In their recent book *Lead Like Jesus,* leadership experts Ken Blanchard and Phil Hodges describe leaders who lead for the sake of their "ego" as "Edging God Out."[3] These are leaders who fully and totally trust in their own power and understanding rather than in God's wisdom and counsel. An unhealthy concoction of pride, fear, self-promotion, and self-protection prevent such a leader from relying on God. The result is that ego-led leaders play games in which they compare themselves to others and distort any information that might reflect negatively upon them because they feel insecure (e.g., that critic is out to get me; he doesn't know what he's talking about; she's taking it out of context).

What Leaders Are Saying When They Trust God

To say to God, "I trust you," may not require many words. However in these few words a leader is actually saying quite a bit. Here are a few of things that leaders are actually saying when they tell God they will trust his leadership of their lives as they in turn lead others.

There Is More to My Life

Invariably leaders will face setbacks and failures, and in those moments of disappointment and trials they might conclude that their life as a leader has been wasted. They might reason that, since they could not take their followers where they wanted to go, nothing is left for them to do but to give up leading. Such defeatism generally takes hold when the leader has been guided by self-trust rather than by trust in God. When leaders trust God, they know there is more to their life than either past problems or the events of any particular moment.

Trust, like hope, is oriented toward the future. When leaders say they trust God in the moments of disappointments, they are saying there is more to life than the present difficulties. They are saying that what God is doing with them will transcend current events and that their value rests not in their leadership accomplishments but in what God will do with their lives in the future. A leader's life is valuable ultimately because God is doing something with it. Leaders who trust God know this truth. Therefore they do not become discouraged or defeated when they encounter failures and disappointments.

I Can't See the Future

When leaders decide to trust God, they recognize that he is sovereign over all creation and the future. They position their role as a leader within a greater purpose than their own plans. When leaders trust in self, they are confident in their ability to orchestrate future events so that things will work out to their benefit. It is arrogance to think that we know exactly what will happen and exactly how things will happen so that we can maximize the greatest results for own agendas. But leaders who trust God know that only God perfectly controls the future outcome of his plans. Recognizing that God alone is sovereign over the future humbles leaders. Consequently, as unexpected tragedies and distractions occur, leaders who trust in God's sovereignty over the future are protected from being anxious. Such leaders believe that God authorizes events and allows people to experience the circumstances of life as they contribute to God's overarching plans to redeem the world.

Such confidence in God when little of the future can be seen is demonstrated throughout Scripture. Abraham could not see what God had in store for him when he was called to leave the familiar surroundings of Ur and go to a land God would show him, but he went. He could not see why God would command him to offer his own son as a sacrifice, but he trusted. Moses did not know what God would do with his people once they had left Egypt behind, but he led the Israelites out into the wilderness anyway. David could not see what God had in store for his kingship when he sent Samuel out to anoint him, but David trusted that God could take care of the future no matter what events would unfold. Jesus' apostles could not see what would happen to them or to those who confessed their faith in Jesus as the Messiah, but they knew that God's will was going to be done and that they could participate in the spread of God's victorious work over death through Jesus.

Christian leaders who experience longevity as leaders know they do not have to know the future. God knows his plans will be accomplished, and it is enough for Christian leaders to trust in the One who sees all, even when they cannot.

God Is Just

Central to the act of trusting God is the recognition of God's justice. A leader who is trusting God is claiming that despite any personal misfortunes and wrongs, God is just and merciful. This attitude makes the leader trustworthy. We do not trust those who we believe will act unjustly toward us. We are suspicious of such leaders and will not take them into our confidence. We only trust someone whom we expect to act toward us in fairness and justice.

The psalmists often call out to worshipers to trust in God's justice and righteousness:

> The LORD examines the righteous,
>> but the wicked, those who love violence,
>> he hates with a passion. (Ps. 11:5)
> The LORD is gracious and righteous;
>> our God is full of compassion. (Ps. 116:5)
> The LORD is righteous in all his ways
>> and faithful in all he does. (Ps. 145:17)

This confidence and belief in God's commitment to justice should draw worshipers into God's presence and prompt them to expect his forgiveness and discipline. In the same way, Christian leaders who are confident that God is just can stand in their leadership over others and know that whatever challenges arise, God is never going to act against them unjustly but only with compassion.

I'm Going to Live Courageously

The Bible often contrasts trusting God with being fearful. Moses warns the Israelites that after they have entered into the land God has given to them they are not to be afraid of the people in the surrounding nations but instead should trust in God who led them out of Egypt (Deut. 7:17–19). Much later, when Judah was surrounded by her enemies, she was again reminded by God through a prophet to have courage, stand strong, and trust in God to deliver them (2 Chron. 20:13–17). And in a powerful story of resurrection, Jesus tells Jairus, a synagogue leader who receives news that his daughter has died, "Don't be afraid; just believe" (Mark 5:36).

This contrast between fear and faith permeates Scripture for good reasons. When people live fearfully and anxiously, they become morally, emotionally, socially, and spiritually paralyzed. Unhealthy trepidation blinds individuals to the possibilities for personal growth and advancement. On the other hand, courage that arises out of trust in God propels people to take hold of the promises of God and to experience life and death in all of their transformative potential.

This is why leaders cannot be fearful but instead must trust in God, who holds all of life and the future within his hands. Such leaders have an adventurous spirit and are willing to question the status quo in order to discover new truths. Courage mobilizes creativity and innovation to solve problems in fresh and dynamic ways. Leaders harnessed by fear see obstacles and roadblocks only as negatives. But those who lead for a long time trust God's word. They say no to fear and embrace the inevitable challenges that come with leading.

God Can Do More

The apostle Paul was undoubtedly a great Christian leader. He led many nonbelievers to faith in Christ. He challenged dysfunctional churches to align their goals and purposes with God's will. He modeled faithfulness under severe physical pressures, even to the point of his own death. Paul's legacy as a Christian leader is due in no small part in his humble conviction that God was at work in him, "a clay vessel," to do far more than Paul could have done if he had relied only on the strength of his own intellect and passion.

Paul experienced God's work in him allowing him to accomplish outstanding work for Christ, and he wanted others to have the same experience in their walk with God. In prayer-like language, Paul told the Ephesians, "Now to him who is able to do immeasurably more than all we ask or imagine, according to his power that is at work within us, to him be glory in the church and in Christ Jesus throughout all generations, for ever and ever! Amen" (Eph. 3:20–21). What Paul knew God had done in him, he knew God could do in others.

Trusting God's power to transform them is characteristic of longtime leaders. They know that they are not perfect. Their actions and efforts are often inadequate for the task, and they show signs of weakness. But, like Paul, Christian leaders who lead for a long time trust that God can do more in their work of leadership than they could accomplish if they relied solely on themselves. God can take the smallest act of faithfulness and grow it into something that will have deep and profound effects on others for his kingdom. If leaders are submitting and trusting their roles as leaders to God, those roles will not be carried in vain. They will impact lives in ways unimaginable and unforeseen, but ways that are in tune with the symphony God is conducting.

Concluding Thought

Trust is absolutely essential for every leader-follower relationship. A leader has to trust those who follow him or her. Followers have to trust the leader to take them where they want to go. Without an exchange of trust, leadership cannot take place. But trusting God is critical for the Christian leader. Without it, a leader will trust someone or something else. Ultimately the leader may end up trusting only self, and this will be disastrous for the followers. Yet, when leaders trust God, they will display the confidence, assurance, and humility that followers desire and benefit from.

Reality Check (Q/A)

1. What is your opinion of the Joy for Jesus program? Do you think such a program would be accepted and work in your town?
2. How is trust or faith in God and in Jesus central to your relationship with God?
3. What does trusting God entail?
4. Why do you think so few people place total trust in God?
5. Why should leaders trust God?
6. Who are some biblical leaders not mentioned in this chapter who trusted God? What made them leaders?
7. How does trusting God affect long-term leadership?
8. How does EGO affect your ability to lead like Jesus?
9. If you were to pick one of the sayings people tell God when they trust him, which would best describe you? Why?
10. What have you witnessed at church or at work when a leader trusts only self? How is that disastrous for followers? Describe.

Case Study: Trusting God

John Neilsen had been the senior associate minister at the Pearson Community Church for twenty years and was very comfortable in his position. He didn't mind preaching occasionally, but he never wanted to be a senior minister completely in charge of a church. He grew up in a loving Christian family, graduated from a small private college, never questioned his faith, and trusted God in all things. He had married the love of his life, and they had two daughters and a son who were faithful Christians. Life was good, even excellent on certain days.

That is, life was good until last year. Last year in March his dad died. His mother grieved at the loss, and John grieved with her. Then in September she contracted viral pneumonia, was sick for two months, and died the week after Thanksgiving. John was trapped in the grieving process again. He had loved both his parents beyond measure. About the time he was getting over the loss of his mother, in April of this year, his wife was diagnosed with pancreatic cancer. The doctors could not be optimistic about her having much longer to live.

John had dealt with so much sorrow, and his wife's diagnosis was the third blow in so short a time span that it threw him into a tailspin. For the first time in his life, he was dealing with disappointment in God. He had always believed in God's healing power, but he was getting no help or relief despite his prayers. He had lost two dear parents and now had the potential of suddenly losing his wife. He felt extremely let down by God. How could he let all this happen in so short of time? Could he even trust God in the future? Would he ever trust God again? Where was God when he was needed? He certainly didn't think that God was speaking or sending messages by the Holy Spirit to him. Was this a test of some sort?

In his private prayers, John was expressing his despondency, lack of trust, and bewilderment about what was happening. He was requesting peace and understanding, but nothing positive was happening. He was afraid to talk about this situation aloud because of his ministerial position. Besides, he had even chastised others about keeping the faith in some very similar circumstances.

John had always thought God was trustworthy, but now he wasn't so sure. Where were God's grace, faithfulness, and goodness now? And yet John had no sensible alternative. John knew he was being too emotional about his current situation, but he was missing the God he had trusted all his life. Where was this all-wise, all-knowing, all-powerful God? Where was this gracious, merciful, loving God? If the devil was responsible for all these bad things in his life, why wasn't God communicating with him?

1. Have you ever been in a situation where you felt the way associate minister John feels? How did you learn to handle it?
2. Do we have to understand the situation we find ourselves in to be able to trust God? Do we have to trust God no matter what? Explain.
3. If you were one of John's close friends, how would you counsel him? How could you help him get his faith back on track so that he can trust God again?
4. Neither you nor John are Job in the Old Testament, so how can you help John to come out of the moment and help him begin to trust God again?

Notes

[1] Joe Klein, "In God They Trust: Washington Faces a New Challenge: Should It Let the Churches Take Over the Inner Cities?," *The New Yorker*, June 16, 1997.

[2] This quote is attributed to Thomas Shepard and cited by Nathan Hatch and Harry Stout in *Jonathan Edwards and the American Experience* (New York: Oxford, 1988), 49.

[3] Ken Blanchard and Phil Hodges, *Lead Like Jesus: Lessons from the Greatest Leadership Role Model of All Time* (Thomas Nelson, 2008).

CHAPTER 3

Trust Others

Whoever can be trusted with very little can also be trusted with much,
\ and whoever is dishonest with very little will also be dishonest with much.

Luke 16:10

Trust carries clout. Amazon, Kraft Foods, Apple, Southwest Airlines, and 3M have cultivated trust. Bill Hybels, Rick Warren, T. D. Jakes, and Joyce Meyer have too. How about your church leaders?

To increase the possibility of longevity, successful church leaders must learn to create an environment of trust. In fact, trust grows with longevity. Gordon MacDonald, former president of InterVarsity Christian Fellowship, has written, "People will follow you for a while because they picked you. But they'll follow you over the long term because they have learned to trust you."[1] Trust is pivotal to all relationships, and it is nurtured by personal integrity.

Trust is sometimes said to be one of those indescribable qualities of relationships. Feelings such as confidence and the absence of worry indicate that trust exists, and a person's performance record confirms trustworthiness. It also involves the ability, willingness, and permission to correct mistakes or miscommunication. Mistrust equals fear. You may find it difficult to define trust, but you know it when you see it and experience it. Trust is a conviction.

Unfortunately, the topic of trust raises the question of how to rebuild trust in an era of rage. For example, as real income steadily declines, many Americans are outraged by the disparity in pay between executives and average workers. Is it possible to build trust in such situations? Do church boards develop compensation systems that reward the ministerial staff fairly and consistently? Is trust the basis for the drive toward results at your church?

We all make mistakes, hurt others unintentionally, and impact relationships. In such instances, we need to own our role in what happened and create a new atmosphere of openness for trust to be restored. In addition, we should ask ourselves whether we are operating from good intentions or manipulative self-interests. Would *you* trust you? Don't give anyone reason to doubt your trustworthiness. Finally, realize that trust is an action and therefore can be restarted. It's impossible to get trust unless you give trust. Engage in authentic communication practices with the other people.

Trust is usually equated with confidence, reliance, expectation, and hope. Organizations with high trust cultures seem to become more profitable. That is why Arie de Geuss, former head of Shell's Strategic Planning Group, said the key to "sustainable competitive advantage" is having a high-trust culture that empowers an organization to learn faster than its competitors.[2]

Trust, however, involves an element of blind faith (not unlike Danish philosopher Soren Kierkegaard's "leap of faith"). Trust is a positive belief in the honesty, truthfulness, justice, or power of someone else. Blind trust is when you put your total trust in God. How much better off would we be personally if we put our total trust in God and let him do what he knows is best?

Sustained high performance is only possible if high levels of trust exist. Trusted organizations that encourage openness, honesty, and ongoing communication typically have lower turnover rates and higher morale than organizations that do not encourage similar policies.

Have you ever wondered what it would have been like to lead hundreds of thousands of people out of four hundred years of slavery into a desert? Probably a bit like herding cats. Imagine the number of complaints there must have been about food and water, the outcries to go back to slavery because they missed the foods they enjoyed in Egypt, the monotony of traveling aimlessly, the obstinacy in group decision making, or the questions about the leader's judgment. How long do you think it took for Moses to win the trust of his followers? How many times did he have to re-win it?

Moses did indeed have his hands full. Many leaders do. Someone has said that trust is faith; it is absolute, ratified, and consummated. It is a firm belief in someone or something. Winning the respect of others, developing mutual feelings of trust between leaders and followers, and opening clogged lines of communication are the kinds of accomplishments most leaders hope for but few achieve. Healthy, trusting relationships encourage followers to achieve their full potential.

The Development of Trust

Edward M. Bounds, a nineteenth- and early twentieth-century Methodist minister and author, wrote that trust is a venture in faith and its exercise. It is a conscious action.

> Trust sees God doing things here and now. Yea, more. It rises to a lofty eminence, and looking into the invisible and the eternal, realizes that God has done things, and regards them as being already done. Trust brings eternity into the annals and happenings of time, transmutes the substance of hope into the reality of fruition and changes promise into present possession. We know when we trust just as we know when we see, just as we are conscious of our sense of touch. Trust sees, receives, holds. Trust is its own witness.[3]

It seems especially important for leaders to keep three points in mind when attempting to cultivate trust in their followers. *First, there are degrees of confidence in someone trusted.* Our levels of trust increase with time and demonstrations of trustworthiness. For example, when we are working with someone new, we may desire to trust them from the very beginning, but it may not be until a few years of working together when we trust them totally. *Second, some minimal amount of risk is involved in trusting others.* Sometimes it appears risky to reach out to others, but the effort usually results in growth. A leader has to take the risk to reach out and inspire would-be followers to take a risk in order to develop a sense of trust. The trust that inspires prayer is a belief that the Lord can move mountains and cast them into the sea. When an individual you have not delegated responsibility and/or authority to before, now sees himself or herself as being trusted, she or he will respond with high motivation. *Third, congruence is critical in any trusting relationship.* It is easier to trust someone when you can find areas of agreement and harmony. Jesus could spend all night in prayer because he and his father were one. Finding areas of harmony and agreement may require more time with someone new or someone whose behavior seems out of character, but the investment will indeed lead toward congruence.

Confidence

We decide who to trust based on a variety of complicated cues—talking speed, gestures, body language, physical appearance, similarity to ourselves, and our level of comfort with a person. Trust cuts across all social arenas and is the glue that cements good social and working relationships. However, trust is fragile. It grows from experience. Followers often withhold trust until they feel safe and are convinced a leader is trustworthy. Trust cannot be demanded or assumed.

Have you ever considered how much trust Timothy's family must have had in Paul to allow Timothy to go with Paul on his missionary journeys? Or how much trust Philemon had in Paul to accept his runaway slave Onesimus back into service? Or how much trust Paul's followers had that he would personally deliver their money to aid those suffering in Jerusalem? Apparently Paul's word was trusted by many. Could you say the same about your word? Are you trusted by your co-workers?

What about your pastoral staff? Does your church family view them as people of integrity? Do they trust them with children, with counseling, with social media, with money?

God is omnipotent; there is nothing he cannot do. Your confidence in his power and grace is not misplaced. In fact, faith, confidence, and trust all go hand in hand. That is why it should be easy to surrender all to him. He created us, bought us, and wants to be with us throughout eternity. Why then is it so difficult to step out of the boat and start walking on water? Why is it so challenging to believe this promise of God?

> "For I know the plans I have for you," declares the LORD, "plans
> to prosper you and not to harm you, plans to give you hope
> and a future. Then you will call on me and come and pray to
> me, and I will listen to you. You will seek me and find me when
> you seek me with all your heart." (Jer. 29:11–13)

Prayer is one of those ways we search for God and find him. Trust is what we express in the act of praying. When we pray, we believe that God wants our prayer and may grant whatever is prayed for. As Bounds has written:

> The trust which our Lord taught as a condition of effectual
> prayer is not of the head but of the heart. It is trust which
> "doubteth not in his heart." Such trust has the Divine assurance
> that it shall be honored with large and satisfying answers. The
> strong promise of our Lord brings faith down to the present,
> and counts on a present answer.[4]

Trust in people is likewise important. Trust is earned, and when it exists, you enjoy the confidence of all those who follow you. Yet it is tenuous. It is destroyed easily and rebuilt slowly. Many counselors, including television personality Dr. Phil McGraw, say the best predictor of future behavior is past behavior. For instance, in a marriage, it may take a lifetime to rebuild trust after one betrayal. Rebuilding trust, if possible at all, is difficult and time-consuming. Sometimes the risk seems too high to try.

Risk

Trusting is risking. If people lived in a risk-free environment, there would be little need for trust. However, we all test one another's reliability. When professors are preparing to take students for a semester abroad, lots of interviewing takes place to settle on whether each student can honor the values and rules and personalities of the professor and the other students in the group. Good decisions help avoid risk in the kind of environment where everyone has to live together closely for a few months. Time spent in such a setting often results in a group where lifetime friendships are made.

Nowhere in the Bible are we promised that there won't be risks in our lives on this earth. That is why you should "trust in the Lord with all your heart and lean not on your own understanding" (Prov. 3:5). Jesus didn't pray that his disciples would be taken out of the world; rather, he prayed they would be kept safe from Satan (see John 17:15). Later, James wrote that we should count it pure joy when tests and challenges (risks) come at us from all directions (Jas. 1:2–3).

Marital relationships threatened or damaged by infidelity can end in divorce, for example. Couples who are able to work through such an event often do so by taking actions that follow a common pattern:

- Both offender and offended must forgive one another.
- The offender must promise not to repeat the problem and then be accountable for that promise.
- The offended must be willing to support the offender and not bring up the past.
- Both offender and offended should celebrate success and rein-force unity.

Such measures may enable a couple to re-establish trust.

Trust is analogous to "going out on a limb." Movie mogul Samuel Goldwyn was known for his ambition, bad temper, genius for publicity, and his philosophy for operations: "I don't want any yes-men around me. I want everybody to tell me the truth even if it costs them their job." If you had worked for Goldwyn, would you have been willing to take such a risk after you became aware of his philosophy? Could you work under such conditions?

Once the limb of trust is cut, mistrust grows. Followers trust leaders to guide, guard, and direct them. If that trust is betrayed, it will be very difficult to regain their trust or to use any motivation technique to move them to higher ground. Neither leaders nor followers can really trust each other until the other demonstrates their trustworthiness. When trust has been achieved, it should not be squandered easily.

Trust, however, cannot be achieved overnight. Trust is built slowly and reinforced over time. It requires patience. And it is always a two-way street! If leaders want followers to trust and respect them, they in turn must trust and respect their followers. The initiative begins at the top, which requires character and strength. Behaviors that hint at suspicion result in unproductive rifts.

Patience is critical in all relationships but especially in an organizational environment. In a society seeking instant answers (instant trust), patience is needed more than ever. Any betrayal of trust is considered by most people as an egregious violation. When trust is damaged, it is very difficult to repair. In fact, it often takes longer to rebuild trust than it did to establish it.

Congruence

Research into patient, credible, trusting climates suggests that leaders trust followers who provide them with congruent—balanced or in agreement—information. That is, most leaders prefer followers with whom they have accord, harmony, or similar experiences. They seek reinforcement from situations which substantiate their attitudes, beliefs, and values. According to Kevin Ford and James Osterhaus, senior officers with TAG Consulting, organizations and the people in them need to find congruent ways to balance trust and cynicism. As the leader you may need to spend some time identifying the reasons for a person's cynical responses. What are the motives that cause his or her behavior? Is it a personality disposition or trait, genetic endowment or environment? Trust is the ultimate goal;

but because this person has to distrust you, you will need to work with him or her to reach the higher level of a trusting relationship.

When confronted with opposing viewpoints, the leader often does not trust either the follower or the information. When inconsistency is present, many leaders typically avoid and distrust those situations, followers, or information. Cognitive dissonance theory (the absence of consistency, that causes discomfort) suggests that leaders tend to avoid followers who hold attitudes, beliefs, or values dissimilar to their own. They are uneasy with them. Furthermore, these dissimilar individuals frequently are viewed as untrustworthy. If this situation exists in the organization between leaders and followers, there is little hope for a cooperative working condition.

In situations like the cognitive dissonance just described, the existence of inconsistency will often motivate leaders to reduce it so that consistency can be restored. Either leaders or followers could try to reduce the tension resulting from distrust and inconsistency in order to restore trust and consistency. For example, the starting point of resolving trust issues is first to trust yourself. As has often been said, "If you can't trust yourself, how can you ever trust someone else?" Second, you have to give trust to get some back. It is easier when struggling with trust to talk through the issues and remain open to hearing what the other person thinks than to continue to ignore the trust problems before you.

Who will do so, however?

The process of searching for congruence (or balance) enables a leader or a follower to grow in character and trust. The tension, however, will always remain because "balance" is an ideal state (like being "perfect") which can never be actually achieved. Achieving this equilibrium—this euphoric state—is not as important as the process a leader takes in searching for congruence and what happens along the way.

Defensiveness can be an act of protecting one's views and may represent a somewhat hostile, emotional state of mind. There are several causes of defensiveness, including self-image. It is traumatic to have your image challenged, to risk losing the ability to predict, control, and know yourself. In fact, any fear of change can be a basis for defensiveness. If followers perceive a threat, both their perception and subsequent behavior will be affected. Defensiveness also can result from an inability to tolerate differences in others. Although defensiveness is greater in some followers than in others, it does affect the behavior of both leaders and followers involved in a communicative encounter. Thus it can create a very destructive, self-perpetuating cycle.

Trustworthiness

The development of trust via confidence, risk, and congruence results in people, business organizations, or churches being viewed as trustworthy. Those who are dependable, who act with integrity, who deal with conflict quickly, who communicate change early, who are honest and candid, who admit mistakes, and who are sincere and selfless exhibit trustworthiness.

XI Interactive, a media development firm in Georgia, for example, set a goal to "be people and a company that is trusted in the marketplace— one that stands for integrity and sets a standard for it, inspiring others to be always truthful and fair as principles held higher than profit and traditional business goals."[5] Like you; no doubt, they believe trust is the foundation of relationships.

If being trustworthy is the key to building relationships, how do you build and strengthen relationships so that other people know how to act around you, aren't afraid of you, or take you at your word? Get some tips from the following list:

1. Communicate openly, frequently, and with intention.
2. Encourage independence, and expect people to excel in their endeavors
3. Treat people the way you expect to be treated.
4. Exhibit integrity and strong business ethics.
5. Maintain confidences, share credit generously, and validate success or new effort.
6. Mingle, ask non-assumptive questions, make promises only if you can keep them, and seek win/win resolution.
7. Encourage input and feedback, and be clear that respectful feedback is welcome.

8. Be as transparent as possible, don't lie about bad news, and if you can't answer a question, say no.

9. Create social time for your people, and offer them accolades when appropriate.

10. Be truthful, honest, reliable, loyal, not biased or prejudiced, humble, accountable cooperative, just, understanding, accessible, responsive, dependable, sincere, selfless, timely, predictable, respectful, open, compassionate, and growth oriented.

Leaders are held to higher standards than their followers, but being trustworthy doesn't necessarily mean being perfect. They will still make mistakes occasionally in decision-making. However, their trustworthiness will show in their willingness to take responsibility for their errors and make things right. They will work to strengthen relationships between them and their followers.

Supportive, Trusting Relationships

In order to achieve success in the trust-building areas of cultivating confidence, overcoming the fear of risk, and learning how to create congruence, important questions need to be answered.

How can leaders reduce defensiveness in followers?

Where does trust enter the picture?

Why would they want to follow me?

Good questions. Whether anyone follows you may have to do with whether they like you, whether they've seen you make good judgments in the past, or whether you are viewed as a winner. If you don't immediately rack up favorable ratings in all those areas, you may have to convince people to follow you.

One way to persuade others to follow is to convince them to change their ideas and/or behavior. However, know up front that a leader's attempt to change followers may backfire. Often when followers perceive that a leader is attempting to make them change (especially if manipulative tactics are involved), they react in a contrary fashion to preserve their freedom to act or think. Therefore, leaders must provide an open, supportive climate in their organizations. Empathizing, understanding, and being genuine go a long way in reducing defensiveness among your followers.

One place to show supportive behaviors can come in the helping relationship, which is a special form of temporary interaction between a *helper*—someone who has achieved an acceptable level of personal adjustment—and a *helpee*—someone who is experiencing difficulty because they lack certain personal skills of adaptation, coping, and problem-solving.

The primary goal is for the helper to inspire constructive behavioral change. And, although no standard helping-skills classification system exists, there are at least three abilities that facilitate the helping relationship: understanding, support, and action. The helper avoids *evaluating*—judging the relative goodness, appropriateness, effectiveness, or rightness of the helpee's statements. The helper refrains from *interpreting*—teaching, imparting meaning, or implying—what the helpee might or should think. Instead, the helper supports—reassures, pacifies, and reduces the helpee's intensity of feeling. The helper *probes*—gathers further information and provokes further discussion, and queries or understands—and then responds in a manner which assists the helpee to understand what has been said or felt.

The helper-helpee relationship finds ultimate support in the knowledge that God has provided for all our needs. For example: "Seek first his kingdom and his righteousness, and all these things will be given to you as well. Therefore do not worry about tomorrow, for tomorrow will worry about itself. Each day has enough trouble of its own" (Matt. 6:33–34).

For spiritual trusting relationships, for effective communication of ideas, for win-win compromises, and for effective solution of problems, effective leaders provide a supportive, trusting climate for their followers.

Reality Check (Q/A)

1. Why do you think trust carries so much clout in profit and non-profit businesses, government institutions, or churches?
2. Do you agree or disagree that trust is an indescribable quality of relationships? Explain.

3. Why do you think that trust is equated with confidence, reliance, expectation, and hope?

4. Do you agree or disagree that trust involves an element of blind faith? Explain.

5. Why is sustained high performance only possible if high trust exists?

6. If trust in the religious world is a venture in faith, do you think the same is true in the business world? Why or why not?

7. Do you agree or disagree that trust cuts across all social arenas and is the glue that cements good social and working relationships? Why?

8. Why is trusting another person risky?

9. Why do you think it takes so long to rebuild trust in a person, once previous trust has been betrayed?

10. Why do leaders typically avoid and distrust incongruent situations, followers, and information?

11. In your opinion, how is trustworthiness demonstrated by an individual?

12. What are the best techniques you've discovered that show supportive, trusting behaviors?

Case Study: Trusting Others

Kevin O'Leary has been the senior minister of the Cornerstone Church for seven years. It has three hundred fifty members and is located in a large metropolitan city. Cornerstone has two associate ministers, six elders, and twelve deacons. Things have been going well for the church, but nothing spectacular has happened in two years. After Kevin accepted the job and arrived at the church, he discovered that the majority of members were apathetic and unfocused on the church's mission. He has concluded that it is nearly impossible to motivate the church leaders and members.

Kevin decided to implement a new program designed to reach out to young families. He also decided to ask one of the younger couples to build a group of young couples. Kevin then gave the group some suggestions that he thought might be helpful to get the new program up and going.

After a few months, the team began complaining to the elders that they were being manipulated by Kevin to get the new program up and running. In short, they did not think Kevin's suggestions were what the team wanted for the church. They were not as excited about the new program as Kevin was, but they do not want to come off looking like hollow church members who also were ineffective.

The elders concluded that such mistrust among the young couples team could jeopardize the church's growth and development.

1. What step do you think the church leaders should take next?
2. What are some of the mistakes Kevin might have made?
3. Since Kevin's leadership is under scrutiny, why do you think he may not understand how he ended up in this situation?
4. Should Kevin be given the responsibility to solve this problem? Why?
5. What could Kevin do to regain the trust of the team?

Notes

[1] Gordon MacDonald, *Building Below the Waterline* (Peabody, MA: Hendrickson, 2011), 71.

[2] "Arie de Geus," *Wikipedia,* Accessed July 31, 2015, http://en.wikipedia.org/wiki/Arie_de_Geus#cite_note-2/.

[3] Edward M. Bounds, *Necessity of Prayer*, Christian Classics Ethereal Library, Accessed July 31, 2015, http://www.ccel.org/ccel/bounds/necessity.iv.html/.

[4] Bounds, *Necessity of Prayer.*

[5] "Core Value: On Being Trustworthy," *XI Interactive* website, Accessed July 31, 2015, http://www.xiinteractiv.com/core-value-trust.cfm/.

CHAPTER 4

Be Transparent and Authentic

All Scripture is God-breathed and is useful for teaching, rebuking, correcting and training in righteousness, so that the servant of God may be thoroughly equipped for every good work.

2 Timothy 3:16–17

So many people say, "what you see *is* what you get." On one level that statement sometimes seems stubborn and negative, and it sounds as though a person wants to come across as telling us, "That's the way I am, and you can take it or leave it." Such an attitude indicates the person has no desire to change, and if you don't like it, that's your problem. On a different level, "what you see is what you get" can be a positive statement of authenticity and transparency—depending on the tone. It can indicate respect and concern for others and for the common good of the business, church, or other organization. When used in a positive sense, it is a promise that you will receive what you need. It is a guarantee.

After September 11, 2001, most Americans felt the need for an authentic leader, someone to lead them out of fear and into a feeling of safety.

Frank Rich, a writer for the *New York Times Magazine,* penned this about our fears and needs:

> On a day when countless children in America lost their fathers, the rest of us started searching for a father, too. When a nation is under siege, it wants someone to tell us what to do to protect us from bullies, to tell us that everything's O.K. and that it's safe to go home now.[1]

Transparency enhances collaboration and credibility. It typically implies openness, trust, accountability, or vulnerability. When we exhibit such nakedness, we are approachable and are viewed as an integral part of a team, department, or organization. One of the clearest paths to longevity for Christian leaders is built on authenticity and transparency. In order to arrive at transparency and authenticity, however, an understanding of self-esteem and self-image is required.

The Phenomenal Self

One of the fascinating ideas regarding perception is that all of us establish a certain concept of ourselves and then select perceptions that are consistent with that image. In fact, one of the fundamental needs of all people is to maintain and enhance their image of ourselves. Because all of us seek out information that confirms what we already believe, we maintain and enhance our images whether they are good or bad. Some people hire image consultants to help them attain their desired goals. Self-perceptions that are inconsistent with what we believe are unlikely to occur because they would not fit our self-image. Any role we are called to play will nearly always be a function of our image satisfaction.

Shakespeare certainly knew what he was talking about in *Hamlet* when he wrote, "This above all—to thine own self be true." The manner in which we perceive is always organized in some pattern that has meaning to the perceiver. The image based on those interpretations has been called "the phenomenal self." This concept is based on self-image and self-esteem and determines the way we behave, what we see, the ideas we develop, and the objects we accept or reject. It also affects our communication with others.

Self-Esteem

Self-esteem and the quest for identity are evident in nearly everything we do. When leaders depend too much on fear and threats to motivate others, they may ignore their followers' intellectual curiosity, desire to understand, and need for self-esteem. The best working conditions seem to be those that blend tension and acceptance—not so tense that colleagues are afraid to speak out but not so accepting that they never feel challenged. Thus, leaders need to work to help colleagues and followers develop positive self-images regarding their knowledge and skills needed to perform the job.

Self-Image

Helping others analyze their self-image is an important component for longtime leaders. The self-image we carry around in our mind is closely connected with how we behave and learn. In fact, one of the reasons people perform poorly is because they consider themselves unable to execute a task well. They may have the intelligence required for the job but not the positive self-image. Thus they are likely to flounder until they either fail or improve their image. Millions of people apparently are the prisoners of their self-perception; they believe they can do far less than they actually can. As a result, they are unhappy, unproductive, and dissatisfied. Such beliefs adversely affect transparency and authenticity.

If we wish to thrive and have organizations that flourish for a long time, we will endeavor to make ourselves and our organizations as transparent as possible. We will show others our true self. Transparency produces authentic behavior, honesty, and realistic relationships, and it links people to one another. Authenticity and transparency open communication channels, enhance self-esteem and self-image, result in better understanding between and among people, and display the pulse of organizations.

Authenticity

Although we have been using the terms authenticity and transparency as though they are the same, there is a difference. Authenticity is genuineness, reliability, trustworthiness, and honesty with those around you;

while transparency is being open, frank, candid, and easily recognized or detected by those around you.

When Paul wrote that all Scripture "is useful for teaching, rebuking, correcting and training in righteousness" (2 Tim. 3:16), he wanted all to realize how the integrity and unity of the whole Scripture has been authentically revealed. All of Scripture is profitable for proper function of our spiritual body so that we "may be thoroughly equipped for every good work" (2 Tim. 3:17). Paul had already told the Colossians that the old Law was "a shadow of the things that were to come; the reality, however, is found in Christ" (2:17).

The Old Testament is the New Testament concealed, and the New Testament is the Old Testament revealed. That's why the writer of Hebrews could say, "The law is only a shadow of the good things that are coming— not the realities themselves" (10:1). The minister's goal should be to glean from both the Old and New Testaments, because every word of God is profitable for learning and teaching. When the minister is transparent with the all-embracing teachings of the Bible, church members will trust in the authenticity of the comprehensive word of God.

Transparency and authenticity provide solidarity well into the future. Ben G. Jacobi, physics professor and author, defines authenticity as being true and honest to oneself and others, thereby demonstrating an absence of pretense. How you choose to live and lead authentically depends on your perspective on authenticity.[2]

Suzi Pomerantz, executive coach and author, writes, "Authenticity is key to effective leadership, and transparency hinges on authenticity."[3] Therefore, leaders must live and work as authentically as possible. If they do so, they will be effective at satisfying the needs of others. On the other hand, leaders who do not live and work authentically will lose meaning, and so will their followers. To be authentic helps demonstrate to others that the most valuable gift you can give is yourself.

The essential elements of personal authenticity, according to Jacobi, include the following: self-awareness, unbiased self-examination, accurate self-knowledge, reflective judgment, personal responsibility and integrity, genuineness and humility, empathy for others, understanding others, and optimal use of feedback.[4] Other lists include items such as being human, honest, and aware. Such lists may remind you of the Golden Rule: "Do to others what you would have them do to you" (Matt. 7:12).

Consultants, like Carter McNamara, find that authenticity is crucial to their work as well. Though clients expect confidentiality, when a consultant can actually share frank conversation with their client, a productive relationship is formed. McNamara notes that authenticity

1. *Encourages clients to be open, honest, and direct in the here-and-now.* The collaborative consultant wants the client to be as open and honest as possible. The consultant can encourage open and honest behavior in others by modeling that behavior themselves. This helps the consultant to fully understand the client and provide useful feedback that the client will hear, as well.

2. *Builds client's trust and confidence in your relationship.* You can build a strong relationship with your client by showing them that you trust them enough to be able to handle the truth. In turn, they will do the same thing for you. Trust and confidence are critical ingredients for a successful working relationship between you and your client.

3. *Deals with issues before the issues fester.* When people express themselves honestly in the here-and-now, they are much more likely to report issues as soon as they notice them. This ensures that issues are addressed when they occur, rather than festering until they show themselves as major forms of resistance to change during the project.

4. *Considers important "data" about the client's situation.* Information that you gather from your other senses is important data about your client's situation. The more open and honest that you can be about your own perceptions, the more likely that the data from your senses will be accurate. Many times that data can be used to more accurately understand your client's situation.

5. *Ensures organizational change efforts remain relevant, realistic, and flexible.* Plans rarely are implemented as planned. Authentic behavior from your clients helps all parties involved to accurately perceive and talk about any changes in the project so, as a result, plans can be updated with those changes and thereby remain up-to-date.[5]

One place where authenticity may be easily witnessed is in team building. Professor and author David C. Smith has written:

In a nutshell . . . human *authenticity* is realized through participation in the collaborative effort of an empowered team in the workplace. A person's full engagement in the work of the team provides a sense of involvement in something greater than the self; at the same time the team depends upon individual abilities and initiatives for the steady innovation required in the business environment.[6]

When teams are first formed, intergroup dynamics should be understood. Interpersonal communication and decision-making skills will need to be developed. Team members' roles will need to be clarified, and a set of rules will have to be agreed upon. Such teams might be formed to improve communication, cope with change, take advantage of new opportunities, or reach decisions about perplexing problems. A team's goals could be task accomplishment, satisfaction of psychological needs, encouragement of meaningful interactions, or team maintenance and strengthening. These teams might be functional, cross-functional, self-managed, or virtual teams. For such teams to be successful, an atmosphere of honesty, openness, transparency, and authenticity will need to be established from the beginning.

As a team works together, several things become paramount: reaching goal consensus, communicating effectively, identifying outside sources that may influence the team's work, assigning responsibility, learning how to overcome difficulties, and ultimately recognizing results. These components of successful teamwork will occur through focused and authentic discussion, brainstorming, and goal-setting. New ideas will emerge, and team members will develop mutual accountability for goal accomplishment.

Barriers to and attitudes against authenticity somehow must be conquered. Barriers include fear of rejection and failure, social pressures to conform, and a lack of understanding of importance of authenticity. Jacobi cautions that authentic attitudes include the desire to circumvent conflicts and hurt, an unwillingness to admit individual flaws, and the avoidance of constructive collaboration with others.[7] Such resistance must be overcome, according to John Moore, business coach and facilitator, because with authenticity, "the unique creative abilities of human beings can be released to create real value."[8]

During the Republican primaries before the 2012 presidential election, Mitt Romney seemed to have difficulty connecting with people. He had been running organizations for a long time, yet he seemed not to come across to a potential constituency as authentic. Taking note of this situation, Jack and Suzy Welch, opinion writers for *Fortune* magazine, offered words of advice for all leaders wishing to connect authentically to those around them.

> Authentic people are deeply comfortable with themselves; they acknowledge without phoniness where they've come from and who they've become, both the good and the not so good, through life's accidents and their own hard work and ambition. Consider, for example, none less than Oprah, who rose to prominence not by hiding her painful past but by sharing it. And then, once famous, continuing to lay her humanity bare on a daily basis.
>
> Second, authentic people say "I love" a lot, as in "I love March Madness!" You name it, they're emoting about it. By the same token, authentic people also tend to throw around "I hate" quite a bit, as in "I hate people who don't talk at meetings." Who knows why they're so passionate? Maybe being candid gives you self-confidence—you're not hiding anything—and

that self-confidence allows you to be exuberant about your beliefs, values, and opinions. But that's just a theory. All we know is what we've observed forever. When it comes to love and hate, authentic people go big.

Third, authentic people aren't afraid to say, "I've screwed up, and I've been down, and it was awful." Authentic people actually seem to relish describing mistakes in gritty detail. Talking about the AOL-Time Warner deal, Ted Turner once said, "It had to be one of the biggest business mistakes ever made. We went into it half-cocked and unprepared. And a lot of people were wiped out because of it, including me."[9]

Becoming authentic is an individual responsibility, however, and requires a commitment to the process. Unless the leader is authentic in a supportive way, followers might sense an aggressive nature of behavior. The leader could possibly be viewed as demanding, forceful, arrogant, or hostile. Such perceptions of inauthenticity could lead to discomfort with, alienation from, confusion with, or distrust of the leader.

Because of such actions by some leaders, Christian women leaders sometimes find it difficult to be authentic and authoritative. Halee Gray Scott, a faculty member at Wesley Seminary and A. W. Tozer Seminary, recommends three things to women who need to create a culture of candor in their organizations: Remember that authenticity and transparency are different; engage in spiritual formation and grow; and build on solid relationships that will benefit all people. Leaders (male and female) must make sure they are employing authentic communication that is honest, supportive, and respectful. It's never too late to lay hold of your authenticity and share yourself with others.[10]

Transparency

There are many ways to think of leadership, but two of those ways are as power leadership or transparent leadership. In the organizational business world, power leadership is often the way one rises within organizations.

Transparent leadership results in rewarding careers as well, and it makes fewer enemies.

Transparency is the sharing of relevant and timely information, as well as the reason, intent, and strategy of a decision. As someone once said, people don't care about what you know; they want to know you care. Transparency is a process, not an act. The creation of transparency in leaders or within an organization may require changing a way of thinking or one's mind-set, in order to change behavior.

Transparent leaders are able to overcome fear. We must become proactive, not reactive, about implementing transparency in our organizations. But remember, if it is possible to have too little transparency, it also is possible to have too much.

Nine behaviors offer guidelines to building credibility through transparent leadership. These guidelines, according to Karen Walker and Barbara Pagano, can help leaders and organizations become more transparent, trusting, and credible.

1. *Be overwhelmingly honest; tell the truth.* Overwhelming honesty should be delivered with respect and concern for others. Followers should not be left to wonder about hidden agendas. Consistency and truthfulness signal that the rules of the game are the same for everyone and that decisions won't be made arbitrarily.

2. *Gather intelligence; encourage people to speak truth to power.* Asking others for their opinions about something conveys respect and shows that they are valued. It also promotes transparency as a reciprocal agreement. How you frame questions is paramount. How you respond—whether you keep an open mind and a clear head—is vital.

3. *Be composed.* Effective and admirable leadership requires composure. Challenges, stressors, and obstacles are inherent in any organization and in any leader's path; how leaders conduct themselves during the good times and the bad can be indicative of their character, competence, and ultimately, credibility.

Followers expect their leaders to be composed. They are always watching.

4. *Let your guard down; reward contrarians.* Because authenticity or personal transparency ultimately describes the quality of a relationship, leaders must create opportunities in which to engage with their followers, allowing the followers to know them. Find colleagues who, if they disagree, are willing to speak candidly and straight forward; listen to them intently, and create conditions for thinking differently.

5. *Keep promises.* When leaders match their words and actions and do what they say they will do, they place a high value on their commitments.

6. *Admit and properly handle mistakes.* Candor is contagious. How leaders handle mistakes actually may be more important than getting things right the first time. Even with its inherent risks, confessing mistakes signals courage, accountability, and humility. Mistakes are an opportunity to visibly demonstrate a commitment to honesty. (It is a willingness to try, to take a step outside the box, to try a new method, or to take a risk.)

7. *Deliver bad news well.* When sensitive, controversial, or potentially hurtful information is not delivered well, people can feel betrayed, angry, and indignant. Trust is destroyed and relationships suffer. Those on the receiving end usually appreciate bad news that is delivered promptly and with honesty, directness, care, and concern.

8. *Practice having unpleasant conversations; avoid destructive comments.* Language that divides or is otherwise destructive can undermine the whole reasoning behind leadership transparency—to improve relationships, increase trust, and build a credible reputation. Leaders must model and reward language that does not employ inappropriate blame or criticism, us-versus-them attitudes, or talking down. The best leaders learn how to deliver bad news kindly so people don't get unnecessarily hurt.

9. *Show others that you care; build organizational support for transparency.* Leaders must visibly show their followers that they do care, and this is done by developing the followers, recognizing them, and seeking to know and understand them. Leaders need to model openness for followers to fully engage.[11]

Leaders who last for a long time create a culture of candor and transparency that follow the above nine steps in their organizations. They are emotionally and socially intelligent, they provide coaching, and they develop trust.

One of the avenues to walk down to enhance authenticity and transparency is sometimes labeled "getting real." A realistic view of yourself greatly affects the way you live daily—that is, the way you think about yourself, your career, and your relationship to God and others.

Our world is full of people who need to get real. There are those whose track record is spiritually inconsistent. Like Christians in the first century, they should be teachers, but they still need to be spoon-fed (see Hebrews 5:11–12). Jesus was rather harsh to the Pharisees and teachers of the law (see Matthew 23:27–28), labeling them hypocrites who appeared righteous (whitewashed tombs) but inside were wicked and unclean (full of dead men's bones). It certainly makes *us* wonder where we are on our spiritual journey.

Reality Check (Q/A)

1. How does transparency in a leader enhance collaboration and credibility?
2. Do you agree or disagree that the fundamental need of all people is to maintain and enhance the image of ourselves? Why?
3. How would you contrast self-esteem and self-image?
4. How does authenticity and transparency open communication channels, result in better understanding between and among people, and monitor the pulse of organizations?
5. What is the difference between transparency and authenticity?

6. What are the essential elements of personal authenticity?
7. Why do you think authenticity is critical to effective team building?
8. What are some barriers to and attitudes against authenticity that you have experienced or witnessed?
9. What are some of the best ways for a leader to connect authentically to followers?
10. What is your definition of transparent leadership?
11. What are some behaviors you have observed that help build credibility through transparent leadership?
12. How do longtime leaders create a culture of candor and transparency?

Case Study: Transparent Leadership

The First City Church leaders are involved in discussions as to whether to close their doors, sell the building, and start meeting with sister churches. The church began meeting on 1968 and during the years has had seven different preachers. None have ever been able to move the church past an attendance of one hundred individuals. Every time it seemed they were finally going to start to grow, their star would fall. People would move to another city, change churches, or quit going to church.

Since their thirtieth anniversary, the church has continued to slide downward in numbers. No other church in their mid-size town seems to be suffering from persistent low numbers. Two ministers ago, a number of gradually demoralized church members began to question the ineptitude of the minister and the church's leadership. Members were complaining about a lack of information sharing in the way the church was being managed. They were expressing disappointment in the way sermons were being delivered from the pulpit. They felt that secrets were being kept that should be shared.

Based on past observations and experiences, the prayerful leaders thought they were doing the right things: listening to their members, investing time in church development activities, and developing strategic visions. Yet they seemed to fall victim to various items of church life they considered irrelevant. They would admit, however, that because of the budget concerns of the last five years, they had a tendency to play their cards very close to the chest. They assumed that telling too much about the budgeting process would only frighten their members. They chaffed, however, at the lack of trust.

In fact, the leaders felt blindsided by the complaints. They endeavored to focus on what they thought was best for the church; but in the eyes of the members, by not sharing enough information or forming committees to explore the problem, they were apparently ignoring potential areas for growth. This narrow view had set the church on a downward trajectory that neither the preacher nor the leaders could correct.

At their fortieth anniversary, they were at the lowest membership point in the history of the church. More members attended on the very first day they met than were attending church now. Paying the bills had become a challenge. Growth seemed out of the question. The attitudes were disruptive, and there seemed to be no way to sustain things. The leaders were at the point of wondering what to do, whether to pull the plug and disband.

1. Do you sense a lack of loyalty on the part of the members? How large a role do you think the complaints of secrets and not sharing information play in this case?
2. Does the fact that growth has stopped contribute to the members' viewpoint about the minister and leaders? Explain.
3. Is there a chance that they can mend things and move forward, or do you think the best step now is to close the doors and sell the building? Why?
4. If you were called in to First City as a church consultant, what would be the first things you would do?

Notes

[1] Frank Rich, "Close Reading: Elements of War; The Father Figure," *The New York Times Magazine,* Sept. 30, 2001, http://www.nytimes.com/2001/09/30/magazine/the-way-we-live-now-9-30-01-close-reading-elements-of-war-the-father-figure.html/.

[2] Ben G. Jacobi, "The Limits of Authenticity," *Philosophy Now,* February/March 2015, https://philosophynow.org/issues/92/The_Limits_of_Authenticity/.

[3] Suzi Pomerantz, "Transparent Leadership," *Innovative Influence* (blog), Dec. 7, 2008, http://www.suzipomerantz.com/transparent-leadership/.

[4] Jacobi, "Limits of Authenticity."

[5] Carter McNamara, "Authenticity—How to Remain Authentic With Yourself and Others," *Free Management Library* (blog), Accessed July 11, 2015, http://managementhelp.org/personalwellness/authenticity.htm/.

[6] David C. Smith, "Team Building and the Pursuit of Human Authenticity," *Business Ethics Quarterly* 3 no. 1 (January, 1993): 79–85.

[7] Jacobi, "Limits of Authenticity."

[8] John Moore, "Authenticity," in *Beyond Branding: How the New Values of Transparency and Integrity Are Changing the World of Brands,* ed. Nicholas Ind (London: Kogan Page, 2005), 104.

[9] Jack Welch and Suzy Welch, "A Little Advice for Candidate Romney: Let Mitt Be Mitt," *Fortune,* March 21, 2012, http://fortune.com/2012/03/21/a-little-advice-for-candidate-romney-let-mitt-be-mitt/.

[10] Halee Gray Scott, "The Titanic Need for Authentic Leaders," April 18, 2012, http://www.christianitytoday.com/gifted-for-leadership/2012/april/titanic-need-for-authentic-leaders.html/.

[11] Karen Walker and Barbara Pagano, "Transparency: The Clear Path to Leadership Credibility," The Linkage Leader, Accessed July 31, 2015, http://www.transparencyfiji.org/docs/Background%20-%20Transparent%20Leadership.pdf/.

GO THE DISTANCE:
ENDEAVOR

WORK HARD

WELCOME CONSTRUCTIVE CRITICISM

FIND A PURPOSE BIGGER THAN YOURSELF

CHAPTER 5

Work Hard

For even when we were with you we gave you this rule:
"The one who is unwilling to work shall not eat."
We hear that some among you are idle and disruptive.
They are not busy; they are busybodies.
Such people we command and urge in the
Lord Jesus Christ to settle down and earn the food they eat.

2 Thessalonians 3:10–12

If you were reared in a conservative environment, you might have
been taught that laziness is morally wrong. You could have been told you
shouldn't live off the efforts of others. Instead you should develop a strong
work ethic and not depend on welfare. In the words of Vince Lombardi,
former coach of the Green Bay Packers, "The price of success is hard
work, dedication to the job at hand, and the determination that whether
we win or lose, we have applied the best of ourselves to the task at hand."[1]
To do different qualifies you as a slacker. You also may have learned from
your family or teachers or other role models that employers want to hire
people who work hard, and hard workers usually are the first promoted.

Much of our thinking about hard work comes from the Puritan work
ethic. It taught us that if you are diligent and work hard, the world will
respect you, and you can have anything you want. It helps to temper these

statements with the knowledge that "God is not unjust; he will not forget your work and the love you have shown him as you have helped his people and continue to help them" (Heb. 6:10).

The apostle Paul knew the importance of not slacking when he told the Thessalonian church that in order to eat they should work (2 Thess. 3:10–12). They should not provide for those of their number who weren't working because they were lazy. Such people did not deserve food to eat; let them go hungry. Some of the Thessalonians had come to Corinth and told Paul that some Christians there still weren't working. They had not obeyed Paul's teaching. This is why Paul, Silas, and Timothy wrote what they did. The problem was not only that these people did not work but also that they expected other Christians to feed them. They had become busybodies, spending their time meddling in the affairs of other people. Paul urged them to keep on doing what is right and not give up in the struggle against all that was wrong.

No doubt there are many more considerations to factor into a work ethic than just working hard. Having a positive attitude, being professional, caring about colleagues, and serving others go a long way. All of these traits help to distinguish you from others during economic downfall or at promotion time. Consider the following statement from inventor Thomas Edison: "The three essentials to achieve anything worthwhile are, first, hard work; second, stick-to-itiveness; third, common sense."[2] Those who do not possess such virtues likely will not be promoted. The achievers are viewed as reliable, dependable, efficient, honest, accurate, punctual, and diligent. They willingly use their initiative and drive to get the job done well. All these characteristics point toward success and garner the attention of those with more seniority.

Hard work is the foundation for appropriate and successful goal completion. Because a robust work ethic ranks at the top of the list in most chosen professions, Steve Pavlina recommends the following steps to develop such a spirit.

1. Accept the fact that many results require hard work.
2. Notice how self-discipline vs. laziness feels to you.

3. Embrace responsibility.
4. Start your day strongly.
5. Exercise.
6. Tackle a real challenge before lunch.
7. Get to it.
8. Act with good purpose.
9. Condition disciplined habits.
10. Work first, then play.
11. Choose your peers with care.
12. Don't use the Law of Attraction as an excuse for laziness.[3]

A strong work ethic fused with proficiency in your chosen career is a powerful force in any organization, profit or nonprofit. Pavlina, writes about an African gold mine two miles deep: "It cost tens of millions of dollars to construct, but it's one of the most lucrative gold mines ever. These miners tackled a very challenging problem with a lot of hard work, but ultimately it's paying off."[4]

Hard work is whatever challenges you, whether it's on the surface or two miles deep. To further emphasize the idea, Norman Vincent Peale wrote, "Nothing of great value in this life comes easily. The things of highest value sometimes come hard. The gold that has the greatest value lies deepest in the earth, as do the diamonds."[5] Although hard work may sometimes remind us of the curse Adam received in the Garden of Eden, hard work pays off. Strong challenges yield convincing results. A robust work ethic is here to stay.

Sometimes good work-ethic maintenance requires extra effort and sacrifice. If you've ever felt that work never ends and you're at the office all the time, you know the previous statement is true. The book of Proverbs provides insight for us:

All hard work brings a profit, but mere talk leads only to poverty. (14:23)

The sluggard's craving will be the death of him, because his hands refuse to work." (21:25)

> He who works his land will have abundant food, but the one
> who chases fantasies will have his fill of poverty." (28:19)

In fact, the unfailing presumption of Proverbs is that work is vital to living and obtaining the necessities for life. If you need to evaluate your skills and abilities in order to keep a superior work ethic, now is the time to do so. You need to decide whether you're working hard or hardly working.

Working Hard

If you work hard, it is probably because you enjoy what you are doing, and your effort is directed in a fruitful direction. You are experiencing what André Weil, an influential mathematician of the twentieth century, refers to as "the state of lucid exaltation." As he explained, "This feeling may last for hours at a time, even for days. Once you have experienced it, you are eager to repeat it."[6] You are busy and productive because you can focus on the job at hand.

The cover story for the October 3, 2005, issue of *Bloomberg Business Week* was entitled "The Real Reasons You're Working So Hard . . . and what you can do about it." The article suggests that we're all working harder and longer, and many of us are on a frenetic work treadmill that we can't turn off. These findings are revealed:

1. More than 31 percent of college-educated male workers are regularly logging fifty or more hours a week at work, up from 22 percent in 1980.
2. Forty percent of American adults get less than seven hours of sleep on weekdays, up from 31 percent in 2001.
3. About 60 percent of us are sometimes or often rushed at mealtime, and one-third of us wolf down lunch at our desks.
4. Over the past twenty-five years, the Information Revolution has boosted productivity by almost 70 percent.
5. The real wages of the best-educated and best-paid college graduates have risen by more than 30 percent since the 1980s.

6. Fully 25 percent of executives at large companies say their com-munications—voice mail, email, and meetings—are nearly or completely unmanageable.

7. Nearly 40 percent of executives spend a half to a full day per week on communications that are not valuable.[7]

This research into why we are working so hard and so many hours resulted in the following *Business Week* conclusion:

> With so many managers and professionals stuck at work, there is a growing consensus among management gurus that the stuck-at-work epidemic is symptomatic of a serious disorder in the organization of corporations. The problem, in a nut-shell-to-go, is this: Succeeding in today's economy requires lightning-fast reflexes and the ability to communicate and col-laborate across the globe. . . . Unfortunately, the communica-tion, coordination, and teamwork so essential for success these days is being superimposed on a corporate structure that has one leg still in its gray flannel suit.[8]

Lowell Bryan, a McKinsey & Co. director, states: "Professionals are still being managed as if they were in factories, in organizations designed to keep everybody siloed. At less well-run companies, you're struck by how frustrated people are. They work like dogs and are wasting time."[9] You may disagree, but we do know that many people hate work. You could even be one of those individuals. The implication is that no one gets a day off any more. Perhaps this is why God told the Israelites, "Six days do your work, but on the seventh day do not work, so that your ox and your donkey may rest and the slave born in your household, and the alien as well, may be refreshed" (Exod. 23:12).

Is there a way for us to ease the work overload, to reduce time pres-sure? Is hard work overrated? Are we perfectionists, hungry for business, entertained by organizational intrigue, or just addicted to 24/7 schedules? We might wonder, "Is there an off switch?

It would make more sense perhaps, according to Greg Herrick, pastor of the Hillside Community Church in Calgary, Alberta, Canada, if we just accepted the teaching of the Bible on work. Specifically:

1. Accept work as God's divine design for you. (See Gen. 2:15; 2 Thess. 3:10). Work is a necessity; it is God's idea.
2. Be careful of the "grass is greener on the other side of the fence" syndrome. Refusing to work reveals a lack of common sense, and looking for a better job is sometimes chasing a fantasy. Ultimately refusal to work leads to death.
3. Do first things first, according to a plan. Prioritize your work. Determine the primary things first, the things on which all else depends, and then tend to the secondary things.
4. If you're going to work, you might as well work hard. According to Proverbs, hard work brings a profit (14:23a), slack work is valueless (18:9) and leads to poverty (14:23b), and diligent work leads to control of your situation (12:24).
5. Enjoy your work—it's God's plan! Work can be very rewarding, we get encouraged when we say nice things to others, and there is a deep sense of pleasure as we reflect upon a job well done.
6. If you're good at what you do, do not be surprised when others want to see you in action. As time passes, people who have worked wisely and diligently will find themselves rewarded by their labor. Those skilled at what they do will be sought out by others.[10]

Because work is God's idea, it is wise for us to work. The Bible encourages us to be diligent and hardworking (Prov. 14:23), to be skilled at what we do (Prov. 22:29), and to work as though we are working for the Lord (Col. 3:22–24).

Working Smarter

In 2013, the U.S. Bureau of Labor Statistics conducted an American Time Use Survey. They asked thousands of Americans to document how they spend every minute of every day. According to the data gathered, on average, most of us spend twenty hours of each day sleeping (8.2 hours/day), working (7.6 hours/day), and watching television (2.8 hours/day). Does that sound like your typical day? Based on the information above, you might wonder who gets to sleep that much.[11]

Those who conduct research about death and the regrets of those dying often hear comments like, "I wish I hadn't worked so hard," or, "I wish I'd had the courage to live a life true to myself." If the person dying had a job that mattered to them, perhaps they are saying that what they regret is working so hard on things that didn't matter to them. If their work had been meaningful, they probably would not have minded the hard work. At this point in your life, you need to decide if what you are doing really matters to you. If you are working at a job that matters to you, you will be dedicated to your work, your colleagues, and the company.

If you are not currently getting the enjoyment and results from your job that you think you should, here are some tips to apply to your work and life in order to experience top productivity:

1. For accurate accomplishment, assess every detail of the job before starting. Be clear on the goal expected.
2. Develop a plan for action. Make a checklist of what needs to be done so you won't forget anything.
3. Create a vision for the job. The end goal is your direction; the vision is your destination. A vision will help focus team members on where they're headed.
4. Aim for the most important tasks that will focus on yielding the highest impact. Cut out the fluff—things that don't contribute to the job or are not needed.
5. Follow the plan, and do not deviate from it. However, be flexible, because things will come up—sickness, ordered parts that don't fit, unpredicted weather emergencies, or other crises.
6. Work as efficiently as possible by creating an environment to assist work flow, foregoing the tendency for perfectionism, asking for help when needed, delegating when possible, or outsourcing.

7. Watch for ways to improve the work being done. Learn from what others are doing, adapt techniques, and make any adjustment needed.

8. Finish strong. You began with enthusiasm; end the same way. You and everyone else should be happy with what was produced.

Learning to work smarter (not harder) should enhance your work ethic and your longevity. Since we're already working hard to get the results we want, we need to learn how to work smarter to receive the maximum value for our effort. If you can combine working hard with working smart, you should reap high results and value.

Mapping Your Energy

While the advice we have just shared makes everything look easier, we know that everybody has highs and lows during the workday. Jason Fitzpatrick, contributing writer to *Lifehacker,* recommends creating an energy map of your week.[12] The goal is to find patterns in your levels of energy and productivity. Fire up your favorite spreadsheet program and open up a weekly planner, one that has the days along the top and the times along the left, split up into fifteen minute or half hour increments or so. Print off several of these (so that they'll travel with you easily). Then just keep it on your desk where you'll notice it all the time. Instead of using it to plan, though, just write in what you're doing and use a number to describe how productive you feel, with a 10 being as productive as you possibly can be and 0 being asleep. Don't worry about preciseness; just use a number that roughly describes how you feel right then.

If you do this consistently over a bunch of weeks, you'll eventually find that you have a pretty good grasp on the points in the week where your productivity is high (lots of high numbers each week in that time slot) and when it's low (lots of low numbers in that slot).

Your energy map would let you see when you need to alter or decrease windows of lower energy or when to schedule certain tasks. As a leader, this activity will allow you to work smarter not harder and thereby increase your professional longevity. It may seem to be a time waster in the beginning, but as Brian Tracy, chairman and CEO of Brian Tracy International, says, "You have to put in many, many, many tiny efforts that nobody sees or appreciates before you achieve anything worthwhile." Your willingness, diligence, and example of a strong work ethic pays dividends now and in the future.

If you accept this premise of learning via mapping your energy, you also should know that anything you do at work can be improved. Thus your aim should not be just to get something done but to get better at doing what you are doing. Perhaps Paul had that in mind when he told the Ephesian Christians "to live a life worthy of the calling" they had received (4:1). As that letter continues, it is apparent that Paul doesn't believe in perfectionism. He does, however, indicate that changes of heart and commitment can transform the lives of Christians. What is required is a radical change in the way we think and behave. Satan will always challenge us, but if we don't allow him to gain a foothold, we can set aside former ways of thinking and acting. We can "be made new in the attitude" of our minds and "put on the new self, created to be like God in true righteousness and holiness" (4:23–24). Paul offers us a work ethic that should be the standard for every Christian.

As a certain Christian administrator used to say to every person at the end of their yearly personnel evaluations, "Now get back to work, and work harder and better." Good advice.

Reality Check (Q/A)

1. What are the factors you deem most important in a work ethic?
2. How have you personally tried to develop a robust work ethic?
3. Do you agree with the statement that "nothing of great value in this life comes easily"? Why?
4. How would you define and contrast working hard and working smart?
5. What is your opinion of the idea that hard work is overrated? Explain.

6. What are some ways you've discovered to get enjoyment and results from your job?
7. How might working smarter (not harder) enhance your work ethic and longevity?
8. How might an energy map let you see when you need to alter or decrease windows of lower energy or when to schedule certain tasks?

Case Study: Hard Work

James Whalley has been an associate minister at the mid-size Mintz-Hill Church for over six years, serving in a variety of roles. He joined the ministry at Mintz-Hill after completing his Master of Divinity degree from an out-of-state seminary.

He has enjoyed his work immensely, even though it is not always easy. Occasionally a certain clique of church members present a real challenge to what he is trying to accomplish. However, he views this challenge as a great opportunity to get involved in an even broader aspect of church work.

The result has been the development of an enviable work ethic. Hard work and achievement are recognized and rewarded by the senior minister. Thus James has been able to move quickly amidst the fast-paced environment of the church's culture, engage in career and professional development, and respond to new challenges.

He believes a real team spirit thrives among the staff at Mintz-Hill. He relishes the idea of doing something different almost every day. His career progression has been structured and well supported, and he has a clear view of his future career with full support of his boss, the senior minister. The staff believes in one another, teamwork, hard work, continuous improvement, and in supporting and developing one another for the future.

When James considers how his career has developed, he sees not only a lot of work but also a number of good people who have always motivated him to put the bar of achievement higher. Thanks to them he believes that everything is possible if you really want it and are willing to work hard to get it.

1. Why has James been able to build such a positive attitude and a hard-work ethic?
2. Why can James overlook the annoying clique of church members who challenge his activities?
3. What role has the senior minister played in developing a team spirit of hard work and support for staff members? Explain.
4. What advantages do you see that have been motivating to James and the others to put the bar of achievement higher?
5. What could you do to develop an attitude that everything is possible if you really want it and are willing to work hard to get it?

Notes

[1]"Vince Lombardi Quotes," Wisdom-of-the-Wise.com, Accessed July 31, 2015, http://www.wisdom-of-the-wise.com/Vince-Lombardi.htm/.

[2]"Thomas A. Edison Quotes," Brainy Quote, Accessed July 31, 2015, http://www.brainyquote.com/quotes/quotes/t/thomasaed149042.html.

[3]Steve Pavlina, "How to Build a Strong Work-Ethic," February 24, 2014, http://www.stevepavlina.com/blog/2014/02/how-to-build-a-strong-work-ethic/.

[4]Steve Pavlina, "Hard Work Defined," June 8, 2005, http://www.stevepavlina.com/blog/2005/06/self-discipline-hard-work/.

[5]"Norman Vincent Peale Quotations," Woopidoo Business Quotations, Accessed July 11, 2015, http://www.woopidoo.com/business_quotes/authors/norman-vincent-peale/.

[6]Andre Weil and Jennifer Gage, *The Apprenticeship of a Mathematician* (Switzerland: Birkhauser, 1991), 91.

[7]Michael Mandel, with Steve Hamm, Carol Matlack, Christopher Farrell, and Ann Therese Palmer, "The Real Reasons You're Working So Hard," *Bloomberg Business Week* (October 3, 2005), http://www.bloomberg.com/bw/stories/2005-10-02/the-real-reasons-youre-working-so-hard-dot-dot-dot/.

[8]Ibid.

[9]Ibid.

[10]Greg Herrick, "The Teaching of Proverbs on Work (July 2, 2004)," http//:bible.org/article/teaching-proverbs-work/.

[11]U.S. Bureau of Labor Statistics, "American Time Use Survey (June 18, 2014)," http://www.bls.gov/news.release/atus.nro.htm/.

[12]Jason Fitzpatrick, "'Energy Map' Your Work Day to Find Peak Productivity Windows," Lifehacker, August 29, 2009, http://lifehacker.com/#!5369774/energy-map-your-work-day-to-find-peak-productivity-windows/.

CHAPTER 6

Non-Defensive Communication

If you are wise, your wisdom will reward you;
if you are a mocker, you alone will suffer.

Proverbs 9:12

Have you ever worked with someone who was not a morning person, someone who just seemed to wake up mad? Or have you encountered someone whose style is to knock doors down and clean up the mess later? Can you tell tales of a nightmare boss? It may be funny now, but it wasn't at the time. Difficult people do exist at work, at church, or at play. They attack, criticize, undermine your professionalism, or are just obnoxious; they laugh at you or ridicule you. Others make fun of people, stir up dissension, start rumors, or are insensitive toward their associates. They make inappropriate remarks and are harsh when dealing with others. Susan Heathfield, a human resources expert, reminds us that difficult people and situations come in every conceivable variety:

> Some talk constantly and never listen. Others must always
> have the last word. Some coworkers fail to keep commitments.

Others criticize anything that they did not create. Difficult coworkers compete with you for power, privilege, and the spotlight; some go way too far in courting the boss' positive opinion—to your diminishment.

Some coworkers attempt to undermine you, and you constantly feel as if you need to watch your back. Your boss plays favorites and the favored party lords it over you; people form cliques and leave you out.[1]

If we are to endure so that your longevity might be increased, we must learn to deal with disruptive, divisive, critical people. In a working environment, some of the most difficult issues indeed are people. Often for pastors the problem they face is that everybody wants to critique what's going on in the church. As someone once said, any fool can criticize, and most fools do. The result is a dysfunctional, toxic working environment.

When Solomon penned the words we used to begin this chapter—the words about wise individuals and mockers, he knew that unless we keep separate from the ungodly, we will never enjoy the pleasures of holiness. To align ourselves with the wicked is to entertain the possibility of being corrupted by them. Thus we must not only forsake the foolish, but we also must join those who walk in wisdom. There is no other true spiritual life or happiness except in the wisdom and worship of God.

Why People Criticize

Certain individuals, sometimes without realizing it, tear down self-esteem, inflict damage, re-open wounds, and cause pain. If you've ever noticed a negative person walking toward you, and you wished you could cross to the other side of the hallway or the street to escape them, you know what we mean. Critical people are not fun.

People who criticize typically do so for one of several reasons. First, they like you but don't believe in what you are doing, and they think their critique will keep you from being disappointed. Second, they want you to fail because their ego is in the way because they weren't consulted during the planning process. They may think they are the only one who should look like an expert on the subject. Or they are just a wiseacre. Third, they don't want to be out of the loop or left behind. Fourth, they don't like you or believe in you, and they think their criticism is the only way to stop you. It's possible they are jealous, or perhaps they are just a killjoy and belittler. They don't mind hurting you to get you to quit. Whatever their motive may be, their intent is to "bring you down."

You listen to your critic, but the whole time you're thinking, I'll prove you wrong and that will be sweet revenge. And when success occurs, you might even consider singing with Toby Keith, "How do you like me now, now that I'm on my way?"[2] On the other hand, you might remember Samuel Johnson's words: "God Himself, Sir, does not propose to judge a man until his life is over. Why should you and I?"[3]

Criticism and Ego: The "Gift" of Rebuke

Some people believe they have the "gift" of rebuke. However, those who are receiving the challenging correction may wish that gift could be lost in translation. Danielle LaPorte, creator of Fire Starter Sessions for entre-preneurs and WhiteHotTruth.com has written: "Criticism sucks. If you're being rightly criticized, your ego needs to shake it off like a wet dog and keep wagging its tail. And if you're being unjustly dissed, you've *still* got to keep your ego limber so that you can objectively fight for your dignity. Either way, criticism is a call to be your classiest self."[4]

King Ahab discouraged Jehoshaphat from sending for the prophet Micaiah: "There is still one prophet through whom we can inquire of the LORD, but I hate him because he never prophesies anything good about me, but always bad" (1 Kgs. 22:8). Today, rebukers may bombard us with criticism via texting, face-to-face, telephone, or email, or an unsigned letter. Or they might throw a rock through our window or slide a note under our office door. A genuine rebuke, however, would be face-to-face and delivered as truth in love.

Often the thing that makes it so difficult to accept criticism is our own ego. Egotism has been the cause of failure for a number of leaders. They find themselves in a difficult situation and fail to keep their ego in check. Granted, we have to have a certain amount of ego to try to stand before people and lead—to give a sermon, to teach, to inspire, and to believe that with God's help we can build up his church. Satan would like to claw at us and tell us we can't or shouldn't give our lives to these pursuits. He's more than willing to assist our egos in getting out of control.

How can we keep ego under control? John C. Maxwell, author and speaker, recommends four ways: First, *seek feedback*. Actively court outside opinions, and believe what your trusted inner circle is saying. Second, *delegate decisions*. Empower others to contribute experience and knowledge and to exercise independent judgment. After all, you may not know the answer to every situation that occurs. Third, *express gratitude*. Show thankfulness, give credit where credit is due, and appreciate the strengths and merits of others. Fourth, *practice servanthood*. Sacrifice time to serve others. Be willing to make yourself small in order to take on the needs of others.[5] However you approach criticism, remember, you need to do so by being classy.

The War Model

An internationally known communication consultant, Sharon Stand Ellison, believes the traditional method of communication is what she calls the "war model."[6] It increases conflict because the focus is on winning arguments rather than on resolving issues. It leads to defensive reactions because it attacks the emotional part of listeners' brains, the part that controls the "fight or flight" response. People react instinctively instead of rationally. Thus the ability to effectively communicate is at best diminished; many times it is temporarily eliminated. The result is defensiveness and a power struggle.

The solution is to use what Ellison calls the Powerful Non-Defensive Communication (PNDC) model of communication. PDNC requires a person to, first, change key attitudes and, second, shift how we ask questions, that is, to change how we give feedback, express our own thoughts, feelings, and beliefs; to create clear boundaries; and to change intention, tone, body language, and formatting (phrasing).

With PNDC, conflict will be minimized, and you will reach a deeper level of understanding. Examples of PNDC skills would include speaking non-defensively, not responding defensively to others, stating opinions without criticism or persuasion, and setting limits without coercion or ultimatums. How's your PNDC?

Overcoming Defensiveness

Another problem sometimes faced, is defensiveness. To illustrate: Do you often become defensive, angry, or negative when you hear criticism? Defensiveness is destructive to the communication process between people. Instead of seeking understanding, you spend time defending yourself. When such things occur, a conflict can continue to grow and remain unresolved. When you feel accused of something, there are a few ways to keep defensiveness from interfering with understanding. One can adapt the recommendations of John Gottman, a marriage and parenting researcher, for overcoming defensiveness.

1. *Be a good listener.* No longer see the critic's words as an attack; rather see them as information that is strongly expressed, a way to get your attention. Genuinely understand and empathize with the feelings behind the words you hear.
2. *Take responsibility.* Answer your critic with something like, "I really made you angry, didn't I?" Acknowledge that your actions might provoke a response.
3. *Apologize.* A straight-out apology is a strong form of validation that lets your critic know you consider the gripe valid and worth respecting.
4. *Praise and admire.* Remind yourself that your critic's negative qualities don't cancel all the positives of the working relationship you have. Memorize the list below, and season your interactions with genuine praise and admiration.

   - Remove the blame from your comments.
   - Don't criticize the other person's personality.
   - Don't insult, mock, or use sarcasm.
   - Stick with one issue at a time.[7]

Whenever the discussions between or among people are yielding more heat than light, these recommendations will help lessen the emotional volume of words being spoken. In addition, it is helpful for you to ask questions, decide what you think, and then speak. Counting to ten before you open your mouth might also help. You might even wish to consider the source and just brush off the criticism; or practice patience, since people have to be patient with you.

Dealing with Criticism

Evaluative judgments can promote constructive growth, when they are dealt with properly. For criticism to be constructive, three assumptions must be in play. First, trust exists between the critic and the receiver. Second, criticism is valid when both the critic and the criticized interact with the evaluative judgments. Second, criticism can be viewed as appropriate if the critic invites criticism of him or her.

I-statements can be used effectively to offer criticism. Basically an I-statement begins a sentence with the first person singular pronoun "I." These statements are used especially when offering constructive criticism or in dispute resolution. For example: "I feel like . . ." "I think . . ." "When I am criticized, I . . ." "I feel unappreciated when . . ." "I get anxious when . . ." "My concern is . . ."

A pastor might hear from a church member, "Ken, I notice that when you don't wear a tie when preaching, you use a lot of slang and informal asides. (Perception) This seems less dignified to me. (Feeling) Could you possibly give more thought to dressing up a little more on Sunday mornings?" (Action)

The pastor might respond thus, "I do feel more relaxed when I wear an open-necked shirt or sweater when I preach. So it is possible that I may slip into some more comfortable speech patterns. Since most of our members dress business casual, I'm seeking to identify with different targets on different Sundays. However, I will try to be more aware of both segments if that is distracting, but please be patient with me. Thanks for caring enough to talk to me about this matter and for listening so closely.

Are there any particular words I use that bother you or others? I know all of us have triggers that tick us off that we should try to get rid of."

Gregg Walker, a professor of speech communication, provides an excellent summary of how to deal with criticism. He established fourteen guidelines *for the critic* who provides constructive criticism.

1. *Understand why you are offering criticism.* Feel confident that doing so is appropriate to the situation and constructive for the parties involved. Criticism voiced out of self-interest or competition may be destructive.

2. *Engage in perspective taking or role reversal.* As you develop a criticism strategy or response, try to understand the perspective of the person being criticized.

3. *Offer criticism of the person's behavior,* not of her or his "person." Refer to what a person does, not her or his "traits" or "character."

4. *Even though criticism implies evaluation, emphasize description.* Before offering any judgment, describe behavior you see or have experienced.

5. *Focus your criticism on a particular situation rather than general or abstract behavior.* "Index" and "date" your criticism, much like a journalist; deal with who, what, where, and when.

6. *Direct your criticism to the present* ("here and now") *rather than the past* ("there and then").

7. *Emphasize in your criticism your perceptions and feelings.* Indicate what you think and feel about the other's behavior that you have described. Use "I" statements.

8. *Invite a collaborative discussion of consequences rather than offering advice.* Form a partnership to deal with problems. Do not compete with the other party; compete with the other person against the problem.

9. *Keep judgments tentative.* Maintain an "open door" of dialogue rather than presenting your "analysis" or "explanation" of another's behavior.

10. *Present criticism in ways that allow the other party to make decisions.* Do not force criticism on the other. Encourage the other to experience "ownership." People are more likely to comply with solutions that they generate.

11. *Avoid critical overload.* Give the other an amount of critical feedback that she or he can handle or understand at that time.

12. *Focus criticism on behaviors that the other person can change.*

13. *Include in your critical feedback a positive "outlet."* Reinforce positive actions and invite the possibility of change.

14. *Invite the other to present criticism of you.*[8]

Criticism can be an opportunity to improve. It is possible to give and accept criticism with grace and appreciation. Being defensive is not a helpful response; anger can place limits on the thinking and learning processes.

Stephen Crippen, a relationship counselor, provides a helpful example of non-defensive listening:

> To listen non-defensively is another step in human development. It's a major element of emotional maturity, and emotional maturity is a highly adaptive quality in a human being. You think I slighted you, and you know what? I can see why you think that. I was certainly not at my best . . . You think I was being selfish? Well, I think it's true that I've been caught up in my own things lately. . . Why don't . . . we talk more about it?[9]

Constructive criticism can have the benefits of personal growth, emotion, improved relationships, time efficiency, and self-confidence. But only if we listen non-defensively. You can't always limit a difficult person's access to your office. At the same time, you may not want to transfer to a new job in the organization or quit your job.

So you might as well be civil about the situation and demonstrate respect. As Peter Drucker, an influential writer and management consultant, once said, "Good manners are the lubricating oil of organizations."[10]

Leadership is about valuing people and relationships. Good manners and civility, therefore, are indispensable. Frances Hesselbein, president and CEO of the Leader to Leader Institute, says she will challenge anyone to "measure the performance of a team whose work is underscored by trust, civility, and good manners against a team where mistrust, disrespect, and lack of consideration are the rule of the day? If you can indeed measure such a comparison, the civil team will win hands down."[11]

Reality Check (Q/A)

1. How would you describe a difficult person and a difficult situation you have encountered?
2. How have you experienced people who tear down self-esteem, inflict damage, reopen wounds, and cause pain?
3. How would you describe a person you know that seems to have the "gift" of rebuke?
4. What are some ways you have discovered to keep your ego under control?
5. Do you agree or disagree with the "war model" of communication? Why?
6. How do you practice the PDNC model of communication?
7. How have you learned to overcome defensiveness?
8. What have you learned about dealing with criticism?
9. In your communication experiences, have you developed skills of non-defensive communication not featured in the chapter? Explain.
10. Have you learned to practice I-statements? Provide an example of how you have done so.
11. Do you agree or disagree that it is possible to give and accept criticism with grace and appreciation? Explain.
12. What is your opinion on the use of respect and civility in person-to-person communication?

Case Study: Non-Defensive Communication

Jay's leadership as a deacon at church is under scrutiny, and he neither knows nor understands what his fellow deacons see as the problem.

Jay is a deacon at the Slinger Church, a 250-member congregation situated in the suburb of a large metropolitan city. It is shepherded by seven elders and has the potential for rapid growth because of a new infusion of entrepreneurs and small business owners moving into the area. Nearby neighborhoods are being revitalized. Jay was selected as a deacon during the last time the church appointed/confirmed elders and deacons. He was recognized as a leader in his business career, someone who got things done, a person who could help the church grow.

The supporters of Jay as a leader were surprised when they witnessed Jay's style of communication in the deacons' business meetings. One evening as potential changes in the worship services were being discussed, Jay seemed to confront the speakers with verbal sparring matches. He seemed to desire and relish an increase in conflict over items being discussed. His focus seemed bent on winning all arguments rather than resolving the issues. After several confrontations with peers that evening, Henry, the chair of the deacons, noticed that Jay's communication style was leading to defensive reactions by other deacons. Henry began to wonder if Jay was causing a "fight or flight" response in those with whom he was communicating. Was it impossible for Jay to move past an argument in order to resolve issues?

Henry noticed that Jay also was defensive when others spoke back to him, attempting to defend their opinions. Henry sensed that other deacons were beginning to feel bad for one another and were not as excited as they were pre-Jay about church work discussions.

After that evening's observations of Jay's behavior and communicative performance, it was obvious something needed to be done. Henry invited Jay to lunch to discuss the perceived problem. One of Henry's concerns was not knowing how Jay would handle a good-intentioned critique in public.

1. Do you think it's a good idea for Henry to visit with Jay over lunch to discuss his communication style and techniques?
2. What do you think he should recommend to Jay to avoid communication defensiveness and a power struggle, and to minimize conflict in order to reach a deeper level of peace and understanding at the deacons' business meetings?
3. How can Henry practice non-defensive communication during the discussion that will take place at lunch?
4. How should Henry coach Jay to listen and respond nondefensively?

Notes

[1] Susan M. Heathfield, "Rise Above the Fray: Dealing with Difficult People at Work," About Money, Accessed July 11, 2015, http://humanresources.about.com/od /workrelationships/a/difficultpeople.htm/.

[2] Toby Keith, "How Do You Like Me Now," Dreamworks Nashville 459051,1999, CD.

[3] "Samuel Johnson Quotes," Goodreads, Accessed July 11, 2015, http://www .goodreads.com/quotes/642488-god-himself-sir-does-not-propose-to-judge-a-man/.

[4] Danielle Laporte, "11 Tips for Dealing with Criticism," Daniellelaporte (Blog) Accessed July 11, 2015, http://www.daniellelaporte.com/11-tips-for-dealing-with-criticism/.

[5] John C. Maxwell, "Burying Your Ego," *Leadership Wired*, April 24, 2011, http://www .patheos.com/blogs/robertricciardelli/ricciardelli/burying-your-ego-by-john-maxwell/.

[6] Sharon Ellison, *Taking the War Out of Our Words* (Wyatt-Mackensie, 2007).

[7] John Gottman, *Why Marriages Succeed or Fail* (Simon & Schuster, 2012).

[8] Greg Walker, "Dealing with Criticism," Accessed July 11, 2015, http://oregonstate .edu/instruct/comm440-540/criticism.htm/. List used with permission from the author.

[9] Stephen Crippen, "Non-defensive Listening," You: A Blog About You and Me, September 2, 2010, http://www.stephencrippen.com/blog/non-defensive-listening/.

[10] Peter Drucker, *Management: Tasks, Responsibilities, and Practices*, rev. ed. (New York: HarperCollins, 2008), 483.

[11] Frances Hesselbein, *Hesselbein on Leadership* (Jossey-Bass, 2002), 33.

CHAPTER 7

Find a Purpose Bigger Than Yourself

And we know that in all things God works for the good of those who love him, who have been called according to his purpose.

Romans 8:28

Is motivation simply a part of the DNA of longtime leaders? Is it because their circumstances are simply more positive and fulfilling than others? Does it have anything to do with the strength of their support system (such as family, friends, or faith in a higher power or God)? Where does a leader's sustaining motivation come from?

Undoubtedly a leader's motivation can be attributed to a number of different factors. But focus on a purpose that was larger than their own immediate needs was one factor to which the longtime leaders we talked to attributed their longevity. They claimed that what kept energizing them to lead was a desire to see something accomplished that would have a longer effect and more significant impact on peoples' lives than those goals that gave immediate rewards to either them personally or to their organization.

Motivation to lead for a long time closely parallels what others have found to be true in the motivation of many people who acquire financial wealth. In their book *Self-Wealth: Creating Prosperity, Serenity and Balance in Your Life,* authors Mark Yarnell, John Radford, and Valerie Bates argue that those who passionately share their wealth with others are motivated to acquire more wealth for the same purpose.[1] This observation is a significant insight into the mentality and emotional intelligence of high achieving investors as well as accomplished leaders. If you've ever watched the television show "Shark Tank," no doubt you've noticed the happiness the five "sharks" get out of telling of their successes in helping other people with their start-up businesses. Getting to do this is a thrill to them.

In his book *The Shaping of an Effective Leader,* Gayle Beebe describes this same motivational principle as looking for the opportunity to make an ultimate contribution.[2] Seeking ways to make an ultimate contribution to society allows leaders to look beyond the immediacy (and setbacks) of their organization's needs and goals. When leaders are consciously seeking opportunities to make impacts that go far beyond the boundaries of their primary responsibilities, they are more motivated to lead.

Vision Casting

What these authors and the leaders we talked to are saying is that the ability to direct one's life toward a goal that is larger than any immediate personal need lets them cast a much-expanded vision of what the future can look like. Vision casting has long been recognized as a crucial characteristic of leaders. Vision not only affects whether the leader's organization will be successful. It also may determine whether the leader will have the stamina to lead through all the highs and lows that come with leading an organization. Therefore, in order to appreciate the contribution of envisioning rather than simply completing organizational goals, we need to explore more closely what a good vision can do. Three particular aspects deserve attention: the impact of vision on personal effectiveness, the necessity of targeted vision, and harnessing vision to energize change.

Vision Promotes Personal Efficiencies

What makes companies or churches more efficient in the use of their resources? Most business leaders claim that what helps them to align all those resources is a clearly crafted and articulated vision. Business consultant Ken Blanchard and others have recently argued that each organization has a culture that consists of several key elements such as people, values, practices, and behaviors.[3] For the organization to achieve greatness, the organization's vision must focus on these elements and implement all of them in carrying out that vision.

In a similar fashion, a person has aspects of their lives (beliefs, habits, relationships, income, health, etc.) which also must be aligned toward and in service of a vision in order for them to be personally effective. One of the ways that this occurs is that the vision enables the leader to determine what barriers need to be removed in order to move toward the vision. A leader might determine that specific areas where they are spending their money or using their time or investing in relationships do not contribute to the greater vision. Without a greater personal vision of the future, it is easy for leaders to become apathetic about how their time and energy are serving only the organization. They can end up looking back on their professional lives and seeing the sacrifices they made to ensure the success of their organization but feeling personally unfulfilled because their vision for their own life has been unmet. They may have to change jobs and find a new leadership position to fulfill their personal talents or vision.

Vision Must Be Targeted

Creating a personal vision may not seem all that difficult. What some leaders may call a "vision" is nothing more than wishful thinking or a general thought about something they would like. An individual's personal vision has the potential to be effective only if particular choices are made. A good vision will inherently say No to some things while saying Yes to other options.

Burt Nanus contends that if organizational leaders wish to create a compelling sense of direction, they need to ask themselves three questions about whether or not their vision for their company is sufficiently targeted:

1. What are the boundaries to your new vision?
2. What must the vision accomplish? How will you know when it is successful?
3. Which critical items must be addressed in the vision?[41]

These questions are equally important for leaders' own visions of doing something larger than what might be necessary to succeed in their own organizations. Two of the "boundaries" Nanus notes are time and place. How long do you want to give yourself to complete those tasks that will contribute toward that vision? When do you want to see your goal accomplished? Simply saying, "One day I would like to do something about children in poverty," is insufficient. While the desire is noble, the vision is too indefinite and provides no timetable or location for its accomplishment. Better would be a vision which states, "Within five years I want to see the monthly number of children in poverty in my state reduced by half of what it is now," or, "I want to see the number of children in poverty in Ethiopia reduced by three percent each year for the next five years." Even better would be a statement of who is responsible for accomplishing the stated goal. Are you going to do something yourself to make it happen? Are you just going to wish for it, or are you going to pray and give a percentage of your profits to make it happen? Having the "boundary" of a timeline, a location, and a personal commitment gives the vision definition and motivates the envisioner to take specific actions with regards to their calendar and to organizations already at work in those areas.

Other "boundaries" that need to be considered in effective vision-making will involve the use of additional resources, such as people, money, agencies, values, and beliefs. A leader may need to refuse to work with certain people to accomplish their goal because those individuals are distractors or inefficient. Decisions will need to be made about which goals fit most clearly with what the leader believes is good and right. Christian leaders have to evaluate whether the vision they want to achieve is consistent with the values of God's kingdom and God's greater work in the world.

Vision Must Be Harnessed to Energize Change

All visions bring about change. We do not usually talk about having a vision in order to "stay as we are." Visions are forward looking and aim to acquire or experience a reality that is currently absent. Therefore, if a vision is going to be effective, it must lead to change. Leaders who have a vision for their lives that is bigger than the demands of their organizations are propelled to make changes. But what is required from us to make the necessary changes that will strengthen us to last not only in our roles as leaders but also in achieving our greater purposes?

Guidelines for Leading Change

Stephen Harper lays out what he sees as twelve guidelines for leaders who want to lead change in their organization. Seven of those twelve guidelines are particularly helpful for those leaders who are making changes so that they can accomplish a big purpose. Those seven guidelines are:

1. Making changes needs to be a way of life.
2. Making changes requires commitment in all areas.
3. Making changes requires letting go of the past and present.
4. Making changes involves "boiling the frog."
5. Making changes must establish relevance.
6. Making changes means creating early victories.
7. Making changes means competing with oneself.[5]

Let's briefly examine each one to see how they impact the leader's pursuit of a greater vision for their life.

First, life is a constant series of changes. We change clothes, we change channels, we change routes. These changes are hardly disruptive but rather routine and mundane. But other changes require significant attention and planning. The decision to get married, have children, send a child off to college, or take a new job requires careful thought about an array of questions. In these cases, the change can be emotionally taxing and time-consuming even when the expected outcome is highly desirable.

But even though our lives are constantly changing (we all get older, after all), some people view change as threatening and unwanted. This fear of change, however, is seldom seen in leaders. Change is a way of life for them. Change is something they are always initiating. The very concept of a "leader" suggests a person who leads people to change from one place to another. So when it comes to making changes to accomplish big goals for their lives, longtime leaders are already accustomed to embracing change as a friend rather than as an adversary.

The second principle reminds us that the decision to change is meaningless if it is not followed by a commitment to examine all of one's life to see what is not adequately aligned with what needs to happen to bring about that change. A person who wants to end hunger in their neighborhood but is not willing to sacrifice time to organize or implement plans that will provide food constantly is merely wishing change. That person is not leading towards change. But this may very well be the place where so many would-be leaders stay "would-bes" rather than becoming leaders. They are unwilling to make the commitment to bring their finances, relationships, energy, time, and intellect to bear on the ingredients essential to change.

A third reason why change is so unappealing to many people is that they realize that in order to acquire the desired changes they will have to let go of things that have helped to characterize the past and still characterize the present. It has been said that no one likes change except a wet baby.

Fourth, the illustration of the "boiling frog" is quite well known. Try to place a frog in boiling water and the frog will immediately jump out. But put the frog in lukewarm water and then slowly bring the water to a boil and the frog will stay in the water and allow itself to be cooked! When looking at making changes to reach a big goal, changes do not have to be so disruptive that they are immediately seen as painful. Don't spook the frog. Keep changing a few things toward the goal, and over time those changes have the potential of accumulating momentum toward reaching the desired vision.

A fifth aspect of making changes that is often frustrating, especially to those who are not responsible for the decision to initiate the change, are changes that seem irrelevant for reaching the desired goal. Imagine a leader who wants to achieve a vision of raising the academic performance of children in lower-income homes but only concentrates on changing the physical décor of classrooms. Relevancy demands an answer to the question "Why?" When this question is answered clearly and reasonably, the change that is made, even if somewhat unpleasant, is better understood and more likely to be embraced.

Sixth, every leader who embarks on changing circumstances in order to reach a big goal knows the powerful influence of celebrating small victories. We see this playing out all time in those who have a vision to live free of tobacco products. The change to stop smoking is disruptive to most smokers, and the desire to return to the habit can be overwhelming. So in order to keep themselves motivated to stay on course to "kick the habit," past smokers will celebrate the days or anniversaries since they last smoked a cigarette. In those celebrations past smokers are reminded of their vision and rewarded for their perseverance. Similarly a leader can maintain the motivation to pursue their vision when they set up moments when they will have reached a particular goal and they celebrate those achievements. For example, if leaders are trying to increase by 50 percent the number of necessary inoculations for women living in a specific underdeveloped country, their motivation to reach that goal can be fed by celebrating when they have reached goals of increasing inoculations by 10 percent, 25 percent, and 40 percent.

The seventh principle has to do with competing with yourself. Changes that lead to a big goal almost invariably entail changes to surroundings or circumstances. Pursuing "big hairy audacious goals"[6] challenges leaders to compete with themselves and possibly to sacrifice other things they are interested in doing and achieving. We all have limited resources and cannot be everywhere we want to be and do everything that we want done. Leaders must make choices, and this includes saying No to self. Visions to accomplish something bigger than oneself often require leaders to compete with other demands that are in themselves good and valuable but do not contribute towards accomplishing the goal. This internal competition is a constant factor, but if leaders, who often relish with enthusiasm the opportunity to compete with others, will welcome this competition with themselves, then their motivation to complete the goal will be strengthened.

Reality Check (Q/A)

1. Why do you think that the motivation to lead for a long time closely parallels what others have found to be true in people who are motivated to acquire financial wealth?
2. Why is vision casting recognized as a crucial aspect of leadership?
3. What are the three particular aspects of what a good vision can do? Explain each.
4. How has vision promoted your personal efficiencies?
5. What are seven guidelines for leading change? Explain how each one impacts leaders' pursuit of a greater vision for their lives.
6. Why do you think change is so unappealing to many people?
7. Have you ever been in a situation where you felt like a "boiling frog"? Describe.
8. How do changes that lead to a big goal entail changes to surroundings or circumstances?
9. What is a "big hairy audacious goal" for you, your company, or your church?
10. How do visions to accomplish something require leaders to compete with other demands that are in themselves good and valuable?

Case Study: A Bigger Purpose

Richard Bower, 28, had just been named the senior minister at the Southwest Church, third largest congregation in their fellowship. He had been an associate minister of education at Southwest since graduating from college. Even though he had been with the church six years, he knew there would be some members who would say he was too young. He and his wife have two children—a boy and a girl, and they had been praying that someday they would have the opportunity to serve the church as the person primarily responsible for leading the church into the future.

Because of the economic conditions in his state and in the nation, he was aware that the church had been struggling some with congregational giving. He did not know the exact conditions of the budget, especially as it pertained to their support of missionaries. Southwest was supporting three families in the mission field. Last night he attended a budget meeting to give his input about budget planning for next year. The chairperson of the finance committee introduced the session by saying the church was still in the throes of declining revenue. Giving had not picked up in the last quarter, and it looked as though the problem of declining revenue would continue into the coming year. There was much discussion among the members of the committee, but at the conclusion of the meeting, the chairperson dismissed everyone with these words: "We simply have to find ways to do more with less."

On the thirty-minute drive home, Richard began to think about whether there were items in the budget he inherited as the senior minister that could be cut in order to do more with less. Then he began to think about how to inspire the chairpersons of every church committee to embrace a new vision of cutting back on budgetary spending. Was there a way he might get everyone at Southwest to strive toward the new reality of decreased revenue and expenses. Perhaps if he could share a vision of the meaning in even a small increase in giving, he might enlist enough members to commit to a small sacrifice in personal spending for the good of the church.

There certainly were many opportunities for people to respond to charities in the community, and many of the church members worked for organizations that encouraged them to get involved in supporting these various entities. He knew some of these individuals were idealistic about wanting to make a difference in the world. Was there a way to convince these members to concentrate on tithes and forego gifts to other nonprofits for one full year in order to avoid cutting the budget? Could they be persuaded that a willingness to share with others was still a spiritual gift even if they concentrated all monetary contributions to the church, which would still be helping others? What would it take to get more individuals interested in sustaining their healthy church activities? After all, weren't they serving a cause bigger than themselves?

1. What are your thoughts about Richard's musings? Is he on the right track? Discuss.
2. How is it possible to get a church to embrace a new vision of budgetary spending to save commitments made for the year?
3. Is it reasonable for Richard to ask members to commit to tithes first and forego giving outside gifts for one year? Explain.
4. If you had to preach a sermon about budget shortfalls and the problems it can cause for the Southwest Church, how would you approach the topic?

Notes

[1]Mark Yarnell, John Radford, and Valerie Bates, *Self-Wealth: Creating Prosperity, Serenity and Balance in Your Life* (Los Angeles: Paper Chase, 1999).

[2]Gayle Beebe, *The Shaping of an Effective Leader: Eight Formative Principles of Leadership* (Downer's Grove, IL: InterVarsity Press, 2011).

[3]Ken Blanchard, *Leading at a Higher Level: Blanchard on Leadership and Creating High Performing Organizations* (New Jersey: Financial Times Press, 2006).

[4]Burt Nanus, *Visionary Leadership* (San Francisco: Jossey-Bass Publishers, 1995), 71.

[5]Stephen Harper, *The Forward-Focused Organization: Visionary Thinking and Breakthrough Leadership to Create Your Company's Future* (New York: AMACOM, 2001).

[6]James C. Collins and Jerry I. Porras, *Built to Last: Successful Habits of Visionary Companies* (New York: HarperBusiness, 1997), 91-114.

GO THE DISTANCE:
AIM

KEEP FOCUSED ON
WHAT'S ESSENTIAL

SEEK MENTORS
AND PROTÉGÉS

CREATE A NETWORK OF
FRIENDS AND SUPPORTERS

CHAPTER 8

Make the Main Thing the Main Thing

Let us run with perseverance the race marked out for us,
fixing our eyes on Jesus, the pioneer and perfecter of faith.
For the job set before him he endured the cross, scorning its shame,
and sat down at the right hand of the throne of God.

Hebrews 12:2

With all the wisdom that allegedly exists in Washington, DC, do you ever wonder if those with learned analysis and perplexing predictions know anything about keeping the main thing the main thing? Are they competent enough to focus on what is most important to us?

One group cautions that our system of governance is bankrupt, that it is mathematically impossible to balance the budget. A second group predicts that the value of the dollar will crumble, that there will be a global economic breakdown. A third group attempts to convince us of the dangers of global warming. Still another group warns us of the possibility of another civil war in the United States because of the lack of trust between government leaders and citizens. We're left to sift through all the confusing data provided via television, newspapers, and websites in a futile effort to make sense of what's going on.

At the end of the day you might begin to think that Stephen Covey was right when he popularized the statement, "The main thing is to keep the main thing the main thing."[1] While that declaration sounds simple enough, you have to first know what the main thing is, what *your* main thing is. In ministry, you must know what God's main thing is.

Keeping the main thing the main thing is not always easy because there are a myriad of things to do, know, and experience. The world sends us messages that the main things are money, social status, interpersonal relationships, material possessions, physical attributes, monetary portfolio, sexual relationships, sports and recreation, travel, music, art, and expensive alcohol and cuisine. It is estimated that we have forty hours a week of discretionary time to use as we wish. Yet we seem busier than ever. Perhaps we have too many options to choose from. Frequently we seem unable to separate the less important from the more important. We fail in our search to identify the main thing.

Once someone asked Jesus what was the main thing (the greatest commandment). If you were asked, would you know? Jesus replied: "'Love the Lord your God with all your heart and with all your soul and with all your mind.' This is the first and greatest commandment. And the second is like it: 'Love your neighbor as yourself.' All the Law and the Prophets hang on these two commandments" (Matt. 22:37–40).

Love. Everything hangs on love. It is a state of mind, a prevailing attitude that leads to action. In *On Christian Doctrine*, Saint Augustine said: "If it seems to you that you have understood the divine scriptures, or any part of them, in such a way that by this understanding you do not build up this twin love of God and neighbor, then you have not understood" (1.36.40). Does this match the world's main message?

The world's main messages are not always God's main messages. What are we to conclude? Based on our research (as presented in Chapter One) we believe that career longevity is enhanced when you stay focused on and have a passion for keeping the main thing God's main thing. But what is the main thing? Do you know?

In the 1991 movie *City Slickers,* Curly Washburn (Jack Palance) says there is "one thing" that really matters in life. He asks Mitch Robbins (Billy

Crystal) if he knows what the secret to life is. Robbins says, "No, what?" Washburn answers: "One thing, just one thing." Robbins looks puzzled and asks, "That's great, but what's the one thing?" Washburn replies, "That's what you've got to figure out."[2] Isn't it true that "one thing" is what should drive us—passion to discover the main thing?

This we believe: your life is blessed when you keep the main things of life central in your faith and in your spiritual walk, when you don't lose sight of the big picture, or when you keep your eyes on the goal.

The Main Thing

Any number of items could be cataloged as main things: family, friends, travel, financial success, education, church, worship, faith, obedience, evangelism, kingdom work, service to others, prayer, or mentoring others. On your job you may have opportunities to explore, links to follow up, articles to write for church bulletins or professional journals, elder or deacon meetings to attend, personal commitments, a sermon to prepare, or a Bible class lesson to study for. Life will always have distractions. Of all those activities and events you are involved in, for which do you have a driving passion?

Passion

Passion refers to the energy, excitement, and conviction that drive you to excel in your personal, professional, and spiritual life. It causes you to stretch, grow, and create. The more passionate you are about what you do, the more successful you will be in doing it. Those who are most passionate bring the most to their work and lives. Passion identifies victorious leaders. It is one of the characteristics that attract talented and dedicated followers. Passion is contagious because others want to be around passionate people. It creates excitement, enthusiasm, and productivity. They become driven to move forward, stretch beyond their perceived limitations, and grow. Like you, they learn to balance the many demands they face.

If you know your passion or purpose for which you were called, you are zeroed in on the main thing. Realize that choice is a journey, a road you travel. Choosing that road is essential if you desire to live a purposeful life. Passion expands your ministry and its effectiveness. The apostle Paul recognized his passion and was able to discard everything as trash in order to follow Christ more perfectly. He was willing to lose all he once counted as gain. "Whatever were gains to me," Paul said, "I now consider loss for the sake of Christ. What is more, I consider everything a loss because of the surpassing worth of knowing Christ Jesus my Lord, for whose sake I have lost all things. I consider them garbage, that I may gain Christ and be found in him" (Phil. 3:7–9).

What had Paul discovered about his life and heritage that he now considered worthless? Just a few verses earlier Paul enumerated these items: he was "of the people of Israel, of the tribe of Benjamin, a Hebrew of Hebrews" (3:5). He said he had been a Pharisee and was so zealous that he harshly persecuted the church (3:6). He had also obeyed the Law without fault.

What had Paul found that would make him consider all his accomplishments were refuse? His revelation about the main thing in his life was clearly stated to the Corinthians: "For I resolved to know nothing while I was with you except Jesus Christ and him crucified" (1 Cor. 2:2) To further illustrate his discovery and to show the importance of God's love, Paul wrote to the Romans: "I am convinced that neither death nor life, neither angels nor demons, neither the present nor the future, nor any powers, neither height nor depth, nor anything else in all creation, will be able to separate us from the love of God that is in Christ Jesus our Lord" (8:38–39).

Paul's passion was for Christ. It was controlled by Jesus. In contrast, King David's third son Absalom became a leader who could not rein in his passion (see 2 Sam. 13–18). His passion was to avenge the rape of his sister Tamar by killing the rapist Amon, David's first son, two years after the occurrence. Perhaps he felt he had the right since the Mosiac law commanded a rapist to be stoned to death (Deut. 22:25-27). Three years later, he burned the field of Joab because he became angry with the general and needed his attention to relay a message to his father. Perhaps these two events happened because he couldn't get the attention from his father the king that he desired. After his passions for anger and revenge were satisfied, Absalom seems to have focused his passion on rebellious politics, lobbying for the support of those willing to follow him, and raising an army to rebel against his father. Because he could not bridle his passions, he was killed in battle when Joab plunged three javelins into Absalom's heart and ten of Joab's soldiers "struck him and killed him." Leaders today must beware the price of passion gone awry, because even the highest ranking and best-equipped fall into sin.

How different would Absalom's and David's lives have been if both of them had remained focused on God's plans, even with all the distractions around them? How different things might have been if they had maintained their poise and remained resolute in their passion for God's ways. If only they had learned to keep the main thing the main thing.

The passion of followers can be discovered, designed, and developed by leaders. According to Michael Kroth and McKay Christensen researchers of passionate work, the following three-step process can unlock the passion that lies within everyone, thereby achieving extraordinary results.

1. *The discovery process involves finding the kind of work a person can be fervent about.* Four interrelated enablers facilitate this first step: self-awareness, experimentation and change, meditating and reflecting, and imagining.

2. *The design process creates an environment that helps people achieve passion in their work.* Three interrelated enablers facilitate this second step: creating meaningful work, making work fun, and creating a nurturing environment.

3. *The development process helps people put passionate work into action and then sustain it.* Three interrelated enablers facilitate this third step: risking, learning, and building self-value.[3]

The best leaders are those who are passionate about what they do and are able to help others grow and be motivated. Does that sound like you, your ministry, or your organization? Passionate leaders are enthusiastic and create an inspiring vision of what needs to be done. They have learned the main thing and how to focus their passion. In ministry, they are motivated to seek first God's "kingdom and his righteousness" (Matt. 6:33). Their mindset is to no longer be conformed to the world but to be transformed by renewed minds, to be "a living sacrifice, holy and pleasing to God—this is your true and proper worship" (Rom. 12:1–2).

Focus

To maintain a passion requires a centralized focus. That focus may be on the mission, ministry, duties, or responsibilities. Focus is an active process of knowing how to achieve and maintain the primary purpose. Unfortunately, you must realize that the plans you set will in all likelihood be interrupted or tested by someone or something else. However, we should not give up our focus because of distractions. Paul compared Timothy's life to that of a soldier who would not get entangled in civilian affairs (2 Tim. 2:3–4).

Jesus insisted that he always did his Father's will—he never neglected God's will—even when he withdrew from the growing crowds to relax and enjoy a time of silence. He had fed the five thousand and healed the sick of the crowd. He had been confronted by some Pharisees and teachers of the law. When his disciples asked if he knew he had offended the Pharisees with his message, he replied, "Leave them; they are blind guides. If the blind lead the blind, both will fall into a pit" (Matt. 15:14).

Then he left to go to the region of Tyre and Sidon. However, a Canaanite woman from that vicinity came to him, crying out, "Lord, Son of David, have mercy on me! My daughter is suffering terribly from demon possession." Jesus doesn't answer her; the disciples urged him to send her away because she was pestering them. When Jesus rebuffed her by stating that he was sent only to Israel and should not give the bread of salvation to unbelieving dogs, she retorted that "even the dogs eat the crumbs that fall from their master's table." Her response amazed Jesus, and he said, "Woman, you have great faith! Your request is granted." Her daughter was healed immediately. Sometimes the necessity of helping others might be outside our immediate purpose, but because it belongs to the greater purpose of God, it is the right thing to do.

As a contrast, near the end of his life, the Preacher of Ecclesiastes gave up focusing on God's will in order to pursue a number of unrelated goals in a vain attempt to focus on himself. At one point he had reached a high level of success. He said,

> I undertook great projects: I built houses for myself and planted vineyards. I made gardens and parks and planted all kinds of fruit trees in them. I made reservoirs to water groves of flourishing trees. I bought male and female slaves and had other slaves who were born in my house. I owned more herds and flocks than anyone in Jerusalem before me. I amassed silver and gold for myself, and the treasure of kings and provinces. I acquired men and women singers and a harem as well—the delights of the heart of man. I became greater by far than anyone in Jerusalem before me. In all this my wisdom stayed with me. (2:4–9)

Unfortunately the Preacher discovered that "everything was meaningless, a chasing after the wind; nothing was gained under the sun" (2:11b).

What we learn from these two illustrations is that we need to stay focused on God's purpose and the purpose he has for us. Sometimes this involves different challenges, situations, and events which are outside our plans.

Any number of techniques could be listed for focusing and staying on target. To live your life with more of a purpose, create the conditions that will allow you to focus on the main thing. Here are ten tips we believe can make a difference:

1. Set well defined goals that are consistent with your priorities.
2. Develop an actionable plan that is within your area of competence.
3. Make to-do lists and prioritize tasks; do the most important thing first.
4. Force yourself to look outside your comfort zone for the right issues.
5. Control interruptions and remove distractions when possible.
6. Learn to say No to the less significant issues, requests, and demands.

7. Create good work habits, avoid procrastination, and complete everything you start.
8. Pursue excellence (not perfectionism) and vigorously track progress.
9. Communicate what your vision, passion, and focus are to your followers.
10. Take care of yourself and pay attention to your health.

Someone once said that if you hunt two jackrabbits at once, you won't catch either one. Effective leaders determine what really matters and pinpoint their focus. They devote their time and energy to the main objectives and issues. They are then able to make decisions about where to invest time and energy.

Keeping the Main Thing Main

There are many ways to get distracted from the main things besides those already mentioned. There are also special projects, spreading yourself too thin, burnout, and failure. Which distractions are you drawn toward? Which traps do you regularly fall into? Solving the disruption problem is not always easy, regrettably. Here are some guidelines we believe will help in any job situation:

1. Seek support and be willing to delegate both authority and responsibility.
2. Let others do their own jobs; do not accept their monkey (problem) on your back.
3. Narrow the job; figure out which issues and areas will make the greatest impact.
4. Organize the people, culture, and circumstances around you.

To keep the main thing main in ministry, consider these guidelines for developing and sustaining the passion to know, love, serve, and become like Jesus.

1. Remember that God has a purpose for your life.
2. Discover that purpose through prayer and practice.

3. Plan how Jesus can become your consuming passion in life.
4. Practice demonstrating your love for Jesus through love, obedience, and service.
5. Do it now!

While it is true that our passion must occasionally be refocused, remember: the purpose of our life is Jesus. Consider that he is mentioned 1,446 times in the New Testament—ten times more than any other person. Along with many other names, he is called Lord, Messiah, the Way, the Truth, the Life, and Lion of Judah. Yet he was betrayed, rejected, mocked, and abused. He died for our sins. Praise God, he was resurrected. Jesus is the only one worthy of our passion and focus.

If following Christ has sometimes been hard for you and you have wondered how to stay on course, to keep the main thing the main thing, the apostle Paul and Silas provide us with an excellent example in Acts 16:16–34. To stay focused . . .

1. Remember your main objective and keep moving in the right direction.
2. Understand that not everyone believes as you do so they may challenge your beliefs.
3. Live in faith and trust and rely upon God's grace.

We are blessed as Christians to know that Jesus Christ is King, that he is our Savior, and that he is preparing a place in heaven for us to live with him throughout eternity. He is the main thing in all that we do—personally, professionally, and spiritually.

PML

Three letters—PML—help frame the means to concentrate on the main points of life and work. Originally they were proposed by Stephen Covey, Robert Merrill, and Rebecca Merrill. These three letters are a good reminder about our ministry. The letters stand for production, management, and leadership, and they are not equal (hence the graphic reminder in the subhead above). Some of us play all three roles; some concentrate on production, others are good at management, and some are gifted leaders.

Which best describes you—producer, manager, or leader? As you might anticipate, intermittently we spend more time producing than managing and even less time leading. We get caught up in the tyranny of the urgent instead of concentrating on the important. According to Harold Shank, president of Ohio Valley College:

> Managers can lose focus, get weary, or miss the big picture. When they do, production suffers. Leaders help them stay on track. Leaders motivate all to be involved. If the managers lose sight of the vision, then organization turns to chaos. When that happens, people drop out of doing productive work. In the end, the one who might have cast the vision ends up doing most of the management and the bulk of the production.[4]

As a designated, current, or aspiring leader, you must focus on being *the* leader. If you are passionate about leading others toward the main thing, the managers can effectively manage and the producers can efficiently produce. If you wish to increase your career longevity, remember, the main thing is to keep the main thing the main thing.

Reality Check (Q/A)

1. How have you learned to keep the main thing the main thing?
2. Why do you think keeping the main thing the main thing is so difficult?
3. Would you agree that your life is blessed when you keep the main things of life central in your faith and spiritual walk? Discuss.
4. For what activities or events do you have a driving passion? Discuss.
5. How might passion expand your ministry and effectiveness?
6. Have you experienced ways by which your passion has been discovered, designed, or developed by others? Explain.

7. Have you discovered ways by which you can stay focused on your job, purpose, or mission? Explain.
8. What are some ways you might get distracted from the main things of life?
9. How would you describe the main things in all that you do—personally, professionally, and spiritually?
10. At this stage in your career, which best describes you—producer, manager, or leader?

Case Study: Main Things[5]

Shelly Marshall is an associate minister at the Applewood Church, an evangelical Christian church in northern California. He has been with the church for six years. The first four years he served as a youth minister, and the last two as the associate minister for church development. The church has seven hundred fifty members.

Shelly has planned a Thursday-Saturday church leadership team retreat that will occur in two weeks. The emphasis will be on what the team sees as the essentials—the main things, the important aspects of church life—in order to avoid mission drift.

Over the past six years, Shelly has become aware of how focus can shift from important aspects of church life to secondary matters for the sake of expediency. The father of management, Peter Drucker once said, "There is nothing so useless as doing efficiently that which should not be done at all."[6] He recognized that Drucker was a great believer in the difference between effectiveness and efficiency and that management was the act of doing things right, whereas leadership was doing right things.

Shelly also recalled that a former teacher had identified five core tasks of ministry and said that all other elements of church leadership emerge from those five tasks: feed the sheep, guard the flock, discern the will of God, train others, and lead by example. Shelly wondered whether the leadership team at Applewood Church would come up with the same grand essentials, something similar, or something entirely different. The retreat should reveal some interesting information about the future of the church.

1. If the main thing is to keep the main thing the main thing, what do you think is the main thing in ministry?

2. What are the core elements—the main things—of ministry at your church?

3. Do you agree with what has been identified as the main things at your church? Explain.

4. If you were a member of the church leadership team, would you have come up with the same five tasks listed in the case? Or would you have recommended different tasks, and if so, which ones?

5. How might a refocus on a church's core ministry put everything else into a proper perspective?

6. Since the discussions and conclusions at the retreat might be varied and nuanced, what would be your recommendations to Shelly about searching and pushing for answers?

7. What would be your advice to Shelly if the retreat ends without a confirmed list of the main things for Applewood Church?

Notes

[1]Stephen Covey, A. Roger Merrill, and Rebecca R. Merrill, *First Things First* (New York: Free Press, 1996).

[2]*City Slickers*, Directed by Ron Underwood (Beverly Hills, CA: MGM: 1991).

[3]Michael Kroth and McKay Christensen, *Career Development Basics: A Complete How-to Guide to Help You* (Alexandria, VA: ASTD Press, 2009), p. 115.

[4]Harold Shank, "Thoughts About Leadership," July 27, 2010 (Ohio Valley President's Blog) http://www.haroldshank.com/whats-the-point/church-leadership/thoughts-about -leadership/.

[5]Adapted from Marshall Shelley, "The Five Main Things," *Leadership Journal* Vol. 33 No. 4 (Fall 2012), 5.

[6]Peter Drucker, "Quotable Quote," Accessed August 28, 2015, http://www.goodreads .com/quotes/348436-there-is-nothing-so-useless-as-doing-efficiently-that-which/.

CHAPTER 9

Seek Mentors and Protégés

You then, my son, be strong in the grace that is in Christ Jesus. And the things you have heard me say in the presence of many witnesses entrust to reliable men who will also be qualified to teach others.

2 Timothy 2:1–2

One of the greatest gifts a pastor receives for longevity is to have been mentored by another person with skills, experience, and wisdom. Your involvement with aspiring leaders requires an investment of time, but it will never be forgotten by the mentee. A mentor is a wise and trusted counselor or teacher, an influential senior supporter. Good leaders deliberately seek out other possible leaders and then train them for future administrative or pastoral roles. Great leaders not only find these potential, wise, and trusted leaders, but they also mentor them to be great leaders.

The first modern usage of the term "mentor" did not occur until 1699. The French writer Francois Fenelon used "mentor" in a book entitled *Les Aventures de Telemaque (The Adventures of Telemachus)*. The slender plot fills out a gap in Homer's *Odyssey*, recounting the educational travels of

Telemachus, son of Ulysses, accompanied by his tutor, Mentor, who is revealed at the end of the story to be Minerva, goddess of wisdom, in disguise. Thus Mentor became our word "mentor."[1] During the Roman period, Quintilian's *Institutes of Oratory* (an edited version of all twelve books from the 1856 English translation by the Rev. John Selby Watson) recommended that leaders find tutors of impeccable morals and knowledge whom they can imitate, and these chosen teachers should be the best of the best. From the Middle Ages to the Industrial Revolution, apprenticeships served as the way to find a mentor. Typically, the apprentice would live with the mentor for several years while learning a trade.

Today a mentor is usually someone older and more experienced who assists in another person's education and development as a leader. In fact, all leaders have a responsibility to develop leaders of tomorrow—to teach, to demonstrate, to allow a protégé to try, and then to evaluate the attempt. The mentor typically will be perceived to have great relevant knowledge, wisdom, or experience. The protégé is perceived to have less knowledge, wisdom, or experience.

Mentors can be found in many locations: church, work, sports, civic clubs, schools, Chambers of Commerce, or professional associations. Since work consumes at least a third of your life, to make it more productive and satisfying, you should either find a mentor or become one. The general advice, to avoid potential problems, is to seek a mentor of the same sex. You may seek the opposite sex for advice, but to have a mentor who is interested in the long-term development of your life and career, it would be best to have a mentor of your gender.

Mentoring

Although the terms "mentor" and "protégé" are not used in the Bible, we find instances of both. To illustrate:

- Moses and Joshua—Exod. 24:13–14; 33:11; Num. 27:15–23; Deut. 31:7–8
- Elijah and Elisha—1 Kings 19:19–21; 2 Kings 2:9–15
- Jesus and the Twelve—Matt. 4:18–21; 28:19–20

- Paul and Timothy—2 Tim. 1:3–7, 14; 2:1–7; 3:10, 14–15

All mentoring is relationship based. Each mentor and each protégé shares something special with the other person; both provide valuable insights to one another in their walk together. One person is primarily the teacher and the other the student.

Mentoring is more than just spending time together talking over coffee. That type of activity might be a form of advising, not mentoring. Norm Brodsky, a veteran entrepreneur, has written: "A mentor's role is not to advise you but rather to give you a different way of thinking. . . . It's critical that they [his mentees] consider what I say but then make their own decisions."

John C. Maxwell, author and speaker, agrees that good leaders seek out, find, and equip potential leaders to be great leaders. He suggests three stages in the equipping a protégé.

1. *Position Gives You a Platform.* Adding value is the essence of equipping others, and you can add value in any direction: to your superiors, peers, or followers. Obviously, you have the most authority when you're the boss. However, even if you aren't in charge, you have immense capacity to equip others through the ideas and resources you share. When it comes to equipping, proximity matters just as much as hierarchy. You'll naturally influence those closest to you: whether you're above or below them on the organizational chart.
2. *Respect Gives You Permission.* People naturally follow leaders stronger than themselves. That's the Law of Respect. Consequently, people will dismiss your attempts to equip them until they're able to assess whether or not they respect you. Respect is earned over time by demonstrating integrity with people and effectiveness in delivering results.
3. *Likeability Gives You Persuasiveness.* All good equipping relationships are founded on a personal relationship. As your people get to know you and like you, their desire to follow

your direction grows. If they dislike you, they will not want to learn from you, and the equipping process can slow down or even stop.[2]

When you think of equippers and mentees or mentors and protégés in the Bible, who do you think of? Moses and Joshua? Elijah and Elisha? Barnabas and Paul? Paul and Timothy? In each of these two-person relationships, one person initiated the mentoring with an end result in mind. An analysis of these relationships, according to Thomas Addington and Stephen Graves, co-founders of Cornerstone Group Consulting and the Life@Work Company, "can be defined as a mutual relationship with an intentional agenda designed to convey specific content along with life wisdom from one individual to another."[3]

A Mutual Relationship

The most complete example of mentoring in the Bible is probably Jesus and his apostles. For three years he stayed with these twelve individuals to guide and prepare them to take his place as spiritual leaders. They not only learned from him, they experienced him. He mentored them over meals, in small groups, by direct confrontation, in question-and-answer sessions, and along the road. In many ways he epitomized the admonition of Moses about teaching: "So commit yourselves wholeheartedly to these words of mine. Tie them to your hands and wear them on your forehead as reminders. Teach them to your children. Talk about them when you are at home and when you are on the road, when you are going to bed and when you are getting up" (Deut. 11:18–19 NLT).

The apostles at times seemed to be slow learners, but eventually they caught on through repetition, concentration, comprehension, and reflection. They were able to authenticate the messages they were learning and become reliable witnesses.

An Intentional Agenda

When Jesus called the Twelve to come and be with him, his invitation was simple, but the message was profound. "Come, follow me, and I will show you how to fish for people!" (Matt. 4:19 NLT). Slowly but surely he called twelve men to follow, and they all did. No one asked, "Where are we going?" They each dropped what they were doing—fishing, calculating taxes, or resting under a tree—and became his protégés. They had no idea where the finish line might be, but they recognized him as the Messiah and willingly became his apostles. However, Jesus knew where the end line was. "Therefore, go and make disciples of all the nations, baptizing them in the name of the Father and the Son and the Holy Spirit. Teach these new disciples to obey all the commands I have given you. And be sure of this: I am with you always, even to the end of the age" (Matt. 28:19–20 NLT).

Jesus had an intentional agenda, a singular focus on the path he would lead to follow. As a mentor, you also must know where the results lie.

Specific Content and Life Wisdom

The three-year journey with Jesus involved both teaching and doing (on-the-job training). Sometimes he taught them face-to-face, and sometimes he did so with larger groups. Either way, the apostles afterwards had an opportunity to ask questions and probe for deeper meanings. They saw him perform miracles, cast out demons, and heal the sick, the blind, and the lame. They heard him read and quote Scripture. As Addington and Graves say, "During the process, the one being mentored has looked, touched, felt, seen and heard."[4] Jesus' men had a sensory experience during their time with him. They were prepared for reality.

From One Person to Another

The mentor is someone who has a depth of knowledge about specific components of work. The mentor also has life wisdom—personally, professionally, and spiritually. The protégé is teachable, has a desire to learn, is willing to put in the time it takes to learn, and looks forward to sitting at the feet of the chosen mentor. The mentoring may take place via giving advice, discipling, customized tutoring, or serving as an intern. Both the mentor and the protégé bond in a mutual relationship because of their desire to learn and a passion to teach.

How to Find a Mentor or Protégé

When we are thinking about mentors and protégés, it is easy to remember the relationship between Paul and Timothy. Paul provided spiritual teaching, skills for working with churches, a role model worthy of following, and time to practice the knowledge and skills learned. From what we see of Timothy in Scripture, he was young and hungry for guidance, open to learn, willing to observe and follow, and willing to accept responsibility. Paul was eager to have such a person with whom to share his knowledge, wisdom, and experience.

A mentoring relationship normally depends on the type of teaching or discipling you need or want to provide. Gerald Tritle, Vice President of Business Development at Peerless Technologies, has written about faithful mentors and protégés in the business world and builds his model of mentoring relationships on Scripture.

- Corporate mentoring requires that faithful mentors and faithful protégés work together for the good of each other and the company to the glory of God. . . . Mentors must embrace the company's goals as well as their own and must direct their energy toward building up the company. In the same manner, protégés must be faithful to their mentors and to the company's interests, in addition to their own.
- A mentor-protégé relationship is no place for pursuit of self-interest at the expense of what is best for the company. Protégés must prove themselves progressively faithful by following the instruction and impartation of their mentors.[5]

Mentoring has been around for thousands of years, so a potential mentor is nearby. If you are a Timothy looking for a Paul, seek a person who is willing to listen to you and hear what you are saying, to share what you see in his or her life that you would like to have in your life, to cultivate a relationship with you, and to hold you accountable. If you are a Paul—someone who has been around for a number of years and you are seeking a Timothy, seek out that person who is goal-oriented, eager to learn, has initiative and a desire to do more. Don't retire your wisdom; pass it on.

Mentoring Techniques

Mentoring techniques were studied by Bob Aubrey, a management consultant, and Paul Cohen, an editor for the Tom Peters Group. They revealed five major techniques or "wisdom tactics":

1. *Accompanying.* This means making a commitment in a caring way. Accompanying involves taking part in the learning process by taking the path with the learner.
2. *Sowing.* Mentors are often confronted with the difficulty of preparing the learner before he or she is ready to change. Sowing is necessary when you know that what you say may not be understood or even acceptable to learners at first but will make sense and have value to the mentee when the situation requires it.
3. *Catalyzing.* When change reaches a critical level of pressure, learning can jump. Here the mentor chooses to plunge the learner right into change, provoking a different way of thinking, a change in identity, or a re-ordering of values.
4. *Showing.* This is making something understandable, or using your own example to demonstrate a skill or activity. You show what you are talking about; you show by your own behavior.
5. *Harvesting.* Here the mentor focuses on what was learned by experience and how useful this new knowledge is. In short, the mentor helps the protégé "pick the ripe fruit."[6]

Dennis Dowdell, a Presidents Team Member, writes that when he mentors someone in his organization or community, he talks about the Five L's of success: learn, love, laugh, labor, and leave.[7] He places importance on learning something new every day, having a sense of self, finding humor all around us, working hard, and retaining the best people. He, likewise, recommends these five L's as the basic life skills for achievement. In addition, he has developed Four C's as another mnemonic device to help people understand the challenges of leadership: conceptual thinking, creativity, communication, and character. He believes it is important to plan, bring forth new and better ideas to serve, deliver good and bad news equally well, and build strength of character—self-knowledge, self-confidence, and self-expression as well as ethical behavior.

Although different techniques may be used by mentors, it is important to look for teachable moments. Mentoring won't solve all the fundamental issues for leaders and followers, but almost everyone has the need and ability to learn and encourage more, to lift the potentialities of those being lead.

Women Need Mentors

It is especially important that professional women find mentors, someone with whom they can build a mentor-protégé relationship. It was once true that a business woman without a mentor didn't have a prayer for successful leadership. However, the more women have moved into the corporate world, the more likely it is they will find a mentor. Beth Hughes Swanson, manager of editorial communications for Wendy's International Inc., has written, "The bottom line for professional women is that they shouldn't feel desperate if they don't have a traditional business mentor. But in some form or fashion, they should seek out wise and supportive counsel."[8] Unfortunately, as Loventrice Farrow, a communications strategist, points out, studies indicate that women of color continue to face challenges in developing their careers and finding mentors.[9] Still, they should at least seek an advisor, if not a mentor. As Swanson also says: "A traditional mentor may have a multitude of roles, among them teaching, modeling, directing, evaluating and providing feedback to the protégé. These different purposes are forming the backbone for many of the new mentoring approaches attracting women, whether they are entrepreneurs or whether they work in an established business culture."[10]

Other professional women agree. Although they are sometimes recognized as the woman or women behind success because of business acumen, down-to-earth product selling, and being technically savvy, many say they learned their analytical and right-brain skills from other professional women. Mentors can be very important to any leader's success.

Senior executives may seem like ideal mentors, but it is no secret that the very nature of their jobs may limit the time they are able to spend in effective mentoring relationships. There may also not be enough willing and available senior executive mentors to go around. In formal programs, organizations should look beyond senior executives for mentors. Affinity groups seem to provide options for informal mentoring opportunities. Organizations can take advantage of the social networking that takes place in these groups to recruit potential mentors and promote the concept of mentoring.

Barry Bozeman, Regents Professor at Georgian Institute of Technology, and Mary Feeney, professor at the University of Illinois, quarried the following meaning from research about mentoring relationships: "Mentoring is a process for the informal transmission of knowledge, social capital, and the psychosocial support perceived . . . as relevant to work, career or professional development."[11] In addition, research emphasizes that mentoring entails informal face-to-face communication over a sustained period of time.

A mentoring relationship can be an important influence in one's professional development. The war for talent in the business world is always active. It is to one's advantage, therefore, to enhance performance, commitment, skill set, and knowledge. Abraham Maslow, an American psychologist, said it well: "If you deliberately plan on being less than you are capable of being, then I warn you that you'll be unhappy for the rest of your life."[12]

Sponsor

In spite of all the information available on mentors, there are those who believe that in the long run a sponsor might be more effective than a mentor of your personal, ministerial, or organizational life. You might wonder what the difference is, why some believe a sponsor is critical to one's future. Their explanation is that mentors coach you, give advice, and help prepare you for your next position; sponsors go out on a limb for you, open the door to your next job, introduce you to the right people, and make the case for you in those top-level conversations that could make or break your career. Heather Foust-Cummings, senior director of research at Catalyst, says, "A mentor will talk *with* you, but a sponsor will talk *about* you."[13]

Harvard Business Review statistics in 2010 reported that out of a study of four thousand high-level employees, 19 percent of the men, compared with 13 percent of the women, had a sponsor.[14] Sylvia Ann Hewlett, president of the Center for Talent Innovation and co-author of the HBR study, said: "Sponsorship is the only way to get those top appointments."[15] Sponsors make sure you have all the right roles to move onward and upward.

How about you? Are you a potential protégé? Are you ready to be found by a sponsor? Take a look at the following five characteristics of protégés and note your qualifications.

- *Performance Counts.* Great work is a must, and before anyone can take a chance on you, they must see that you're loyal, trustworthy, and dependable. These executives are betting their own reputations on your career.
- *Find Your Star Power.* Don't assume that putting your head down and doing your work will get you noticed. You need to become a known entity. Volunteer for bigger assignments, attend conferences, and become active in your profession.
- *Don't Force It.* Most relationships evolve naturally and won't happen if you flat out ask someone to be your sponsor. Hedge your bets against your sponsor leaving the company by nurturing relationships with multiple people.
- *Be Confident.* If you're worried that you're not qualified for that major assignment or concerned about your two-year-old at home, do not share your honest ambivalence with a sponsor. Show you're ready for an opportunity. When you get feedback, handle it with a thick skin and be prepared to act on advice given.
- *Return the Favor.* Unlike a mentor, a sponsor will expect your loyal support in return. A sponsor benefits, too, from the "power

of the posse" to build his or her own career. After all, no one gets to the top alone.[16]

One of the most valuable assets for men and women in their careers is to have a good mentor. So, as a mentor, sponsor, or protégé, are you ready to take the next step—to give or seek wise counsel?

Reality Check (Q/A)

1. Do you agree with the statement that good leaders seek out, find, and equip potential leaders to be great leaders? Why?
2. Do you have a mentor(s)? Did you find them? Or did they volunteer to be your mentor? Describe how it came to be.
3. Do you agree that mentoring involves a mutual relationship, an intentional agenda, and specific content and life wisdom? Explain.
4. What have you learned about how to find a mentor or protégé?
5. What mentoring techniques have you discovered that you believe are "wisdom tactics"?
6. How have you used the Five L's of success?
7. How have you used the Four C's to help people understand the challenges of leadership?
8. Do you agree or disagree that women need mentors more than men need mentors? Why?
9. When might a sponsor be more effective than a mentor?
10. Do you agree with the five characteristics of protégés? Why?

Case Study: Mentoring

Ben is in his fourth year as a young, associate minister at Paradise Church. He is working under Frank, a well-respected senior minister whose spiritual influence on church members is well known in the community. Ben's work has been conscientious but unproductive. He feels stuck and has tried to discuss this with Frank, but Frank tells him to just keep trying. "You'll get results eventually," is all Frank ever tells Ben.

Recognizing that mentoring is of the utmost importance in the training of new, young ministers, the elders at Paradise set a policy that senior ministers are to act as formal mentors for interns and younger ministers. Ben has therefore relied on Frank and has not formed a personal relationship with anyone else on staff. He thinks that because of Frank's other activities Frank is not giving him the attention he needs.

Frank has a personal interest in educational materials, and he has developed a video program that generates a potential for online learning for other churches and their members. He uses the video series to teach classes at Paradise. His videos are a hit with all the teachers at church. Frank realizes that the videos have broad appeal, and he has a talent for marketing the videos while sharing the programs with Paradise free of charge.

Ben's concern is that Frank is not providing him with the guidance he needs. Ben often ends up answering calls about the videos and troubleshooting curricular programs for Frank. This type of work has left Ben feeling overwhelmed, but he doesn't want to appear unwilling to help. Ben knows that Frank, owing to his excellent reputation and extensive contacts in the field, could be very helpful to him learning the realities of the ministerial life. He also hopes that in the next year Frank will arrange for him to preach more often, as well as to speak at national conferences.

When Ben discusses the future possibilities and personal needs for mentoring, in the hope that Frank will intercede in some way, Frank refuses to get involved and says, "It is not my responsibility." Ben is quite frustrated and has decided to visit with a senior faculty member in the Bible department at a local university. Ben studied with this professor while obtaining his M.Div. degree. The faculty member works with other graduate students and churches and seems to take an active part in fostering not only his students but also their careers.

1. It appears early on that Frank may have low expectations of Ben, or that he is, for other reasons, relatively passive with regard to Ben's progress. What is Ben's responsibility in this situation?

2. Frank has many responsibilities as a senior minister, but he is also running a business. What is his responsibility as Ben's supervisory and mentor?

3. Ben's work on behalf of Frank's video venture is diverting his attention from meeting his own ministerial responsibilities. Whose responsibility is it to ensure that this does not happen?

4. Does the Bible professor have any responsibility after Ben comes to talk to him?

5. Is Frank acting reasonably in response to Ben's requests for help and mentoring? What other options does Ben have in attempting to handle this situation?

Notes

[1] Gordon F. Shea, *Mentoring*, rev. ed. (Menlo Park, CA: Crisp Publications,1997).

[2] John C. Maxwell, "The Three Stages of Equipping," http://www.johnmaxwell.com /cms/images/uploads/pdf/3_Stages_of_Equipping[1].pdf/.

[3] Thomas Addington and Stephen Graves, "The Four Elements of Mentoring," *The Life@Work Journal* 1,4 (September 1998): 24.

[4] Ibid.

[5] Gerald Title, "The Wisdom of Business Mentorship," *Business Reform* 2, 6 (November/December 2002): 12-15.

[6] Robert Aubrey and Paul M. Cohen, *Working Wisdom: Timeless Skills and Vanguard Strategies for Learning Organizations* (San Francisco: Jossey-Bass,1995).

[7] Dennis Dowdell, "Mentoring for the Future," *Leader to Leader* (Winter 2001): 9-11.

[8] Beth Hughes Swanson, "Seeking Wise Counsel," *Life@Work Journal* 1, 4 (September 1998): 33-35.

[9] Loventrice Farrow, "The Experiences of Minority Women Leaders as Mentees in U.S. Organizations," *Emerging Leadership Journeys* 1,2 (2008): 25-42.

[10] Swanson, 36-37.

[11] Barry Bozeman and Mark K. Feeney, "Toward A Useful Theory of Mentoring," *Administration & Society* 39,6 (2007): 719-739.

[12] Abraham Maslow, *The Farther Reaches of Human Nature* (New York: Viking Press, 1971), 36.

[13] Jennifer Alserver, "Want to Move Up? Get a Sponsor," *Fortune* (May 21, 2012): 54.

[14] Ibid.

[15] Ibid.

[16] Ibid.

CHAPTER 10

Create a Network of Friends and Supporters

As iron sharpens iron, so one man sharpens another.

Proverbs 27:17

S everal years ago *Usa Today* ran an astonishing claim about the importance of friends. According to a report from the George Washington Medical Center in Washington DC, women who once had moderate forms of breast cancer were able, with a network of supportive friends, to cut the recurrence of cancer over a seven-year period by 60 percent. Conversely, women whose breast cancer were in remission and had less than three supportive friends were 60 percent more likely to see their cancer return and for many of these women their cancer will lead to death.[1] The conclusion of the researchers was that the moral and psychological support a patient received from their friends made a tremendous difference in their ability to fight their disease. Having friends can literally save a person's life.

Not surprisingly, something similar is true about longtime leaders. Leaders who experience longevity in their roles as leaders have a supportive network of friends. John Maxwell correctly observed that "every leader's potential is determined by the people closest to him."[2] Who leaders surround themselves with matters. If leaders surround themselves with people of wisdom, they are often led away from disastrous decisions. If leaders are surrounded by peers motivated and passionate about their work, they are inspired even when they feel emotionally or physically depleted. Leaders who gather around themselves people driven towards excellence are themselves energized to do the same. It matters who leaders turn to for support.

Throughout the Bible the concept is repeated that human beings need support from others. It is a fundamental part of being human. After God created Adam, he said that it was not good for man to be alone (Gen. 2:18). So he created Eve to be Adam's partner in cultivating and caring for the garden. In the Israelite wisdom tradition, the sage stated that "two are better than one, because they have a good reward for their toil. For if they fall, one will lift up the other; but woe to one who is alone and falls and does not have another to help" (Eccl. 4:9–10). In an effort to illustrate the wisdom of having support in one's life, the sage compares friends to a rope. "A threefold cord is not easily broken" (Eccl. 4:12 DRB). The point is obvious: We all need other people in our lives because we will inevitably experience setbacks, discouragements, obstacles, loss, and even failures. But these experiences do not break us when we experience them with the support of friends.

The same biblical principle is equally true for those who lead. Leading can often feel like a lonely and treacherous adventure, but it is a myth to think that successful leaders are loners. Loners might make good characters for movie plots, but in the real world effective, long lasting leaders have others by their side helping them in many ways. Leaders who have friends to turn to in their time of need are given new strength to face their battles. They are given a renewed breath of life when the burden of leadership seems particularly heavy. All longtime leaders know that there is invaluable strength in the intimate community of friendship.

Friendship and Supporters among Biblical Leaders

In Luke's version of the parable about the man who built a house, Jesus specifies that the man dug into the ground and laid a foundation on a rock, and because of that the house was able to stand when the flood came against it (Luke 6:48). Jesus didn't tell this parable to instruct his disciples about leadership. He told it to explain that a wise disciple listens and obeys Christ's teachings in order to be prepared for the day of final judgment. A truth in that wisdom, however, equally applies to leaders who want to last. Leaders who spend time cultivating supporters have a solid foundation for those times when opposition, disappointment, and disaster strike.

Several times in Scripture godly leaders appear who have friends or others supporting them. Whether it is Prince Jonathan giving David friendship and confidence (1 Sam. 19–20), Jesus' inner circle of disciples of Peter, James, and John (Matt. 17:1–13; 26:37–46), or the network of friends and benefactors who supported Paul's missionary travels, a constant feature of biblical leaders who honor God is they have individuals beside them sharing their struggle and providing support.

How Do Friends and Supporters Contribute to a Leader's Longevity?

There are undoubtedly several reasons why a circle of friends and supporters will help leaders to last. One obvious reason is that good supporters remind leaders why they are good leaders. One of the huge dangers every leader must face is self-doubt. When leaders make mistakes, as all will invariably do at some time, some are tempted to be overly critical of themselves. They begin to doubt that they have the necessary intuition to lead. They doubt they will have the stamina to keep going. They will wonder whether or not the sacrifices they are making will be worth it in the end.

This is where good supporters are absolutely crucial. Wise friends, associates, and colleagues come alongside leaders and remind them of their strengths. They gently and firmly point out those qualities and characteristics that were seen in them at the beginning and that are still there. They reassure leaders that those attributes that are essential in a leadership role have not left them and that they are still capable of leading others.

What Kind of Supporters Do Leaders Need?

Basically every leader needs three kinds of support. The first support they need is followers. There is no such thing as a follower-less leader. One is a leader because they have people who believe in them and will go where the leader takes them. Supporters like this should never be taken for granted. Leaders will constantly need to cultivate the quality and depth of these relationships.

The second type of support every leader will need is benefactors. These are the people who have authority over them. Nearly every leader has someone to whom they must answer. In businesses it maybe a superior or a board or a group of stockholders to whom the leader must give an account for their actions. In a church or ministry context, the leader (in addition to always having to answer first to God) more than likely will have to answer to a church's governing leadership or a pastor or to the congregation collectively. Benefactors are the people who gave leaders the opportunity to lead others, and they are a crucial part of the support system the leader will need.

Just as leaders will have to constantly cultivate the relationship they have with their followers, so too they must give ongoing careful attention to those who have authority over them and empower them to lead. When I (John) was given the responsibility to serve a large church as their preaching minister, one piece of advice I was given by a preacher who had served successfully for a long time was to make sure that I spend one-on-one time with each of the church's fourteen elders. My relationship with them would have a huge impact on my ability to gain support from the congregation.

The final kind of supporter leaders require is what I will call "enablers." Recently the word *enabler* has come to be used in a negative sense. We often talk about people who "enable" others to stay in unhealthy or self-destructive habits. But the word *enable* can be used positively to describe people who can assist a leader to succeed or endure.

There are five types of leadership enablers. Let's take a brief look at each and see how their role contributes to a leader's longevity.

The Honest Critic

Everyone needs an honest critic. Most people do not like to hear criticism, even when it is given with the best intentions. But, for a leader, an honest critic is an absolute necessity. Leaders who have withstood the floods of complaints and anger from others have been aided by friends who have been willing to tell them the truth even when it hurts. The sage got it right when he wrote, "Well meant are the wounds a friend inflicts, but profuse are the kisses of an enemy" (Prov. 27:6 NRSV). In other words, a friend or a supporter who has to tell the leader something unpleasant or critical may well know that their criticism is going to be painful, but they are willing even to inflict a "wound" on their friend if it will help that friend in the long run. People who do not truly care for us may lavish us with praise, but a friend who supports us will be willing to speak the truth about us even if momentarily it hurts. Longtime leaders surround themselves with people they can trust to tell them what they need to hear about themselves, even if that information is painful to hear. Poor leaders are satisfied to be encircled with people who will only give them lip-service praise and positive strokes to their ego.

The Grounder

One of the common pitfalls of leaders is that their egos become inflated because of the power and responsibility they have. Inflated ego can blind leaders to their own self-destructive and other-destructive behaviors.

What longtime leaders benefit from are individuals who "ground" them by reminding them that the universe does not rotate around them. By gently (and often humorously) reminding the leader of their faults and weaknesses, "grounders" help leaders keep perspective on who they really are. They help leaders not to think of themselves more highly than they ought to think.

The Healer

Leaders, like everyone else in the world, make mistakes. They misstep. They say things they later regret. They do things they wish they could take back. They make decisions that were not thought through. In these moments leaders who are conscientious hurt because of what they have done wrong.

A healer is one who comes alongside the leader and speaks words to soothe their pain. They remind their friend that the mistakes they have made are not unknown in the world. They are not the first to make a wrong turn, and they will not be the last to do so. The healer enters into the leader's heart with words and deeds to repair the damage that has been done to a leader's spirit.

The Distractor

Some distractions are good. While it is true that it can be disastrous for leaders to be distracted constantly from their main goals and objectives by tasks that should be delegated to others, it is also true that leaders need some distractions from the demands of their role. Leaders who last have friends and supporters who know when to step in and take that leader off into some activity that will rejuvenate their energy.

The distraction can be something as simple as taking them away to eat in a place they enjoy. The distraction could involve more time away from the office, such as an afternoon for recreation or a long trip. Whatever the activity is, the task of these good distractors is to get leaders involved in doing something different and unrelated to the immediate responsibilities they have.

The Interferer

Leaders are public people. By this we mean that leaders must connect with those who follow them and with those who could potentially follow them. As such, followers and potential followers will want leaders' attention in order to make them aware of the concerns and agendas they have. In fact, leaders who project themselves as open to and appreciative of new ideas and helpful suggestions could find themselves bombarded with many well-intentioned thoughts, complaints, and bits of advice that could unwittingly take up their time. This is where a wise interferer can step in as support to a leader. They perceive the potential threat to the leader's time and come between the leader and those who want to give advice.

Often wise leaders, especially those in large organizations, will have the foresight to know that many people will want to talk directly to them and that there is not enough expendable time to hear from all of them. They therefore put in place associates and colleagues who will run this kind of inference for them. In other organizations leaders will depend upon their inner circle of friends and supporters to step into this role.

Moses has this kind of experience with his father-in-law Jethro. In the Exodus saga, Moses has successfully led the Israelites out of Egypt. Now in the wilderness they are protected by God from their enemies. Jethro hears of Moses's success and comes out to see Moses and the situation for himself. In addition to confirming God's deliverance of the Israelites, he also witnesses that Moses is hearing all the people's desires to know what God wants them to do in their individual situations. Jethro wisely concludes that this arrangement is not good. If Moses continues on this path of judging cases all on his own, he will wear himself out (Exod. 18:17–18). Jethro advises Moses to get some "interferers" in the form of judges who can hear all of the minor requests. He urges Moses to make these arrangements so that Moses will be able to endure (Exod. 18:23).

Godly leaders who last for a long time, like Moses, cultivate a network of people who will help them balance their time. The interferer's job is to help the leader balance that time between the leader's focus on the priority tasks to be completed and the leader's need to be receptive and open to the ideas, thoughts and concerns of those who follow them.

A Final Reminder about Friends and Supporters

It should be clear by now that friends and supporters are crucial to the longevity of those in leadership. But before we conclude this chapter, let us look at one truth leaders cannot ignore. Even leaders' most ardent friends and supporters can let them down.

It is unreasonable and unfair for leaders to expect that their inner circle of support will behave without blemish. Friends make mistakes, too. Supporters will misstep. Leaders are not perfect, nor are their friends. While building that network of people who will aid you in effective leadership, continue to offer the same grace and understanding to them when they let you down that you want from them when you let them down.

Reality Check (Q/A)

1. Have you been in a situation to observe (or hear about) how friends have saved a person's life (metaphorically speaking)? Explain.
2. Do you agree that leaders who are surrounded by peers who are motivated and passionate about their work are inspired even when they feel emotionally or physically depleted? Discuss.
3. Can you think of a time when you needed support from family, friends, or colleagues? If so, what was the end result?
4. What is the expected outcome for leaders who spend time to cultivate supporters?
5. How do friends and supporters contribute to a leader's longevity?
6. What three kinds of supporters do leaders need? Explain each.
7. What are the five types of leadership enablers? Explain each.
8. Have you ever had to inflict a "wound" on someone to help them in the long run? Describe.
9. Why do you think poor leaders are satisfied with being surrounded by people who will only give them lip-service praise and positive ego strokes?
10. Have you ever been in a situation where your friends and/or supporters let you down? Discuss.

Case Study: Friends and Supporters

Breanna Stanford, 25, works with the youth group at the Oak Knoll Church. Her focus primarily is on the pre-teen and teenage girls in the church. Oak Knoll is a large church in a large city and is sensitive to the needs of the suburban areas around Oak Knoll, especially as it concerns less fortunate individuals. Breanna is in her third year of work, having been at Oak Knoll since her graduation from a nearby private college.

Yesterday she had her yearly evaluation by the senior minister. Although the evaluation meeting set her at ease as they talked about her strengths in working with the female students at church, the senior minister then began to challenge her thinking about personal growth and the future. Breanna had always considered herself to be fascinated by other people and what they did. She was on social media frequently with friends from high school and college.

However, she was being critiqued for showing no signs of networking with people outside the congregation who could be of help to her career. She was also questioned about her participation in local charitable causes. She was asked how often she invited newcomers to the youth group out to lunch or after school for ice cream or a soft drink to get to know them better, how often she visited them at various school activities. What surprised her most, though, was being asked how well connected she was to get things done through the relationships she had not only with teenagers but also with parents and outsiders. Then the senior minister wanted to know her sources of information and support that would help her gain future professional traction.

As a wrap-up, he said, "I want you to think about these things, start working on the types of activities I'm asking about. Look for some youth minister training workshops or lectures that work within your budget. Spend some time searching for books, magazines, or journals that might be helpful. Then let's set a date to meet again formally in three months to see what processes you've put in place and how you are proceeding. Six months from now, let's see what changes you've made in your work and other related activities that might make a difference in how you are building friendships and networks for the good of your work as a youth minister and as a longtime worker in the Kingdom."

Breanna left the meeting wondering if she was getting a message that old friends might be a waste of time if they could not contribute to career and future.

1. Why do you think Breanna was so surprised to be evaluated on the basis of how she was building a personal network?

2. What are some immediate steps you would encourage Breanna to begin taking?

3. How would you encourage her to focus more on building relationships that would support her career in ministry?

4. If you were the elder or deacon with oversight responsibility of the youth group and Breanna came to you seeking advice, how would you help her be even more effective and have broader impact as she continues to want to be involved in church ministry?

Notes:

[1] Marilyn Elias, "Friends May Make Breast Cancer More Survivable," *USA Today,* March 8, 2001.

[2] John C. Maxwell, *The 21 Irrefutable Laws of Leadership: Follow Them and People Will Follow You* (Nashville: Thomas Nelson, 1998).

GO THE DISTANCE:
MOTIVATE

DEVELOP COMMUNITY, COLLABORATION, AND CONSENSUS

COMMUNICATE RESPONSIBLY

BE AN ENGAGED LISTENER

CHAPTER 11

Develop Community, Collaboration, and Consensus

As a prisoner for the Lord, then, I urge you to live a life worthy of the calling you have received. Be completely humble and gentle; be patient, bearing with one another in love. Make every effort to keep the unity of the Spirit through the bond of peace.

Ephesians 4:1–3

Building a community of believers was a goal of the early church. Those first converts to Christianity gathered together every day because they wanted to be together, to share in their spiritual journey. That early community was not perfect, however; it was not without the risk of hurt. Do you remember the lack of honesty displayed by Ananias and Sapphira, the murmuring of the Greek-speaking Jews (or Hellenists) because their widows were not being fed fairly, or the jealousy of the Sadducees toward the apostolic church leaders? In spite of these problems, this early church was something radically new, and it served as an example to unbelievers—especially because it included women in their midst.

Community is a natural process. The trinity (or triune) represents a spiritual community; the creation of the first man and woman represents a human community. The first human community had the responsibility of taking care of one another and of Eden. The fall of Adam and Eve, however, broke the special relationship they had with God. They were no longer as safe or as comfortable as they had been. Life as a community became difficult.

As that first family grew and became larger, physical communities began to develop and spread due to geographical preferences, travel and trade routes, food resources, different languages, and customs. Cities were built, towers were erected, and sin became a common misfortune of community life. Covenantal relationships with God began to disappear; relationships broke down. As British novelist and Christian apologist C. S. Lewis said, "Aim at heaven and you will get earth thrown in. Aim at earth and you will get nothing."[1] Different values and morals crept in, and the residents of these communities began to operate on some unwholesome principles. They were rebellious, unable to obey God's law fully. They were lost. Interests became diverse and were motivated by selfishness.

The building of a human community of positive and spiritual relationships was on a downhill slope. It would take the birth and death of Jesus Christ to create hope for the Gentiles. A new motivation for living and working together and serving others was provided, and this dynamic is still a global need in business, church, government, nonprofits, and education.

Building Community

Community building is a process of constructing unselfish relationships among people around a common interest. Any number of activities could be used to build community in a congregation—church potlucks, adult sport leagues, book review clubs, civic clubs, brothers keepers groups, or mentoring relationships. The process of building a community involves letting people find what works and what doesn't. In this process, communication among participants is critical.

American psychiatrist and author M. Scott Peck created a four-stage model of community building: pseudocommunity, chaos, emptiness, and community.[2] This process is distinctive, similar to a laboratory for experimentation to find what works.

The *Pseudocommunity Stage* is the beginning. People are on their best behavior; they avoid being personal and skirt conflict and controversy. Little communication occurs until the members become vulnerable about self and to their surroundings, until they drop their guard and begin to share information about themselves. Once transparency is revealed, safety, trust, and respect usually result.

The *Chaos Stage* is one of conflict. Prejudices, opinions, and judgments clutter the air space. Anger sometimes results as people attempt to heal or convert one another. Scapegoats are sought. Change advice is offered. Group norms are explored. A state of anxiety is created, and personal contemplativeness takes place as people begin to concentrate on their own behaviors and actions. We see this stage in business and in churches when battle lines are drawn around key issues and people are taking sides and trying to get people to join their cause.

The *Emptiness Stage* is one of "emptying" personal baggage that interferes with the process of personal growth. People become quieter and for the first time really start to listen to one another. Personal authenticity is revealed. A peace settles over the members, gratitude is expressed, and a collective consciousness emerges.

The *Community Stage* is one of appreciation for the process and the participants. The result is a feeling of wholeness and acceptance of self and others. People are recognized and appreciated for who they are—warts and all.

Other models and processes of community development can be found. But Jerry L. Hampton, relationship workshops specialist suggests that in the above process "people find an inner part of themselves being moved to speak by a force greater than they can define" in order to restore a balance in their relationships. He says the general characteristics of these "community people" appear to be acceptance, compassion, understanding, authenticity, peacefulness, respect, and love.[3]

Once community has been achieved, collaborative teams can be established and a culture of assignment ownership can be built.

Collaboration

Collaboration is necessary for effective decision making. It occurs when two or more people, teams, or organizations with a shared purpose and direction meet to undertake a work project. In fact, highly productive people tend to have wide networks and are great collaborators. They get much done by bouncing ideas off colleagues and clients. More specifically, according to authors Paul W. Mattessich, Marta Murray-Close, and Barbara R. Monsey, collaboration is "a mutually beneficial and well-defined relationship entered into by two or more [people or] organizations. The relationship includes a commitment to mutual relationships and goals; a jointly developed structure and shared responsibility; mutual authority and accountability for success; and sharing of resources and rewards."[4]

Susan Cain, a writer for the *New York Times,* says: "Virtually all American workers now spend time on teams, and some 70 percent inhabit open-plan offices, in which no one has 'a room of one's own.' During the last decades, the average amount of space allotted to each employee shrank 300 square feet, from 500 square feet in the 1970s to 200 square feet in 2010."[5] You might wonder if performance plunges when space shrinks. Cain would argue that in the age of collaboration one of the things that makes people more creative and productive is privacy. Apparently 200 square feet of office space yields not only better privacy but also higher productivity.

If collaboration is to result in high performance, a number of components are essential (see Table 10.1). The items listed below seem to encompass all of the necessary elements for collaboration.

Table 10.1

Successful Collaboration Components	
Trust between leader and members	Adequate resources
Integrity and honesty of leader	Team ownership of projects
Competence and effectiveness of leader	Joint assumption of risks and resources
Appropriate cross section of members	Realistic expectations
Mutual respect among members	Open and frequent communication

Shared vision, goals, and norms	Awareness of why the group exists
Formalized roles of members	Hope in participation results
Self-accountability	Recognition for accomplishments
Sharing of power and decision making	Service to one another
Acceptance of full responsibility	

The list of why some teams don't work well together and thereby fail is probably a longer list than the one above, however. Think of the last team you were a part of that didn't work well together. Why? What made the team dysfunctional? What elements above were missing from the working arrangement? Often a lack of success could center on trust, expectations, mutual respect, or lack of communication. More frequently, however, the problem may be the ineffectiveness of the leader. If the team had collaborated internally, they would have been able to compete externally.

Collaborative efforts offer a number of advantages. Therefore, team leaders must recognize that success in working with others will depend on involving everyone as peers. The benefits of doing so include the following: Decisions are faster, of higher quality, and customer driven; and decisions are made on the basis of principle rather than power or personality. Cycle time is substantially reduced, non-value-adding work is eliminated, and the productive capacity of the workforce doubles. Strategic alliances succeed, return on investment increases dramatically, and the span of control increases substantially. The workforce takes on full responsibility for the success of the organization, conflict is reduced as trust is built, and any fear is gone. Change is seen as a positive opportunity.

A number of leadership theories, studies, and research findings will help those who lead the collaboration process. For example, David D. Chrislip and Carl E. Larson, authors on the subjects of teamwork, perspectives on communication, and collaborative leadership, say that collaborative efforts are recommended because more traditional leadership methods have failed.[6] See if you agree.

Traditional leadership involves having the power to direct, drive, instruct, and control members. The focus is on task and not on relationships. In contrast, *transactional leadership* is a model of a dynamic relationship by Edwin P. Hollander, an organizational social psychologist.[7] It involves ongoing interpersonal evaluations by members and leaders. Those individuals who are deemed trustworthy are allowed to innovate and recommend new strategies.

Contingency leadership was postulated by Fred E. Fiedler, a researcher in industrial and organizational psychology. He said that the influence of a leader depends on how well liked and respected the leader is, the degree of clarity and structure of the task assigned, and the amount of authority the leader holds by virtue of formal or designated position.[8]

Transformational leadership motivates people to do more than they envision by raising awareness of different values and transcending self-interests. It provides individual consideration and stimulates people to think in new ways. James M. Kouzes, the Dean's Executive Professor of Leadership, and Barry Z. Bozeman, professor of leadership at Santa Clara University, popularized transformational leadership in an exhaustive study which called for five actions: challenge the process, inspire a shared vision, enable others to act, model the way, and encourage the heart.[9]

Charismatic leadership, according to Robert J. House, a professor of management at the University of Pennsylvania, and Boas Shamir, professor of sociology at the Hebrew University, results when leaders use their personal characteristics and views to create obligations in their followers.[10] They possess a high level of certainty in self and a willingness to impose that certainty on others. For example, the apostle Peter was charismatic because he displayed poise and optimism—*confidence*—as a buoyant communicator, he had *conviction,* he knew where he was going and what he had to say, and he spoke straight from his heart.[11]

Likewise, Peter focused not on himself, but on others. He magnetically made *connection* with his audience. He exuded warmth and love—*compassion.* He gave people practical answers to their needs. His personality and passion drew people to him. In contrast, the pride and selfishness of Ahab and Jezebel were not magnets to draw people to them. They preferred manipulation and deceit.

By contrast, according to *The Maxwell Leadership Bible,* Abigail was able to use her relational skills to take charge of a situation that her

husband Nabal had exacerbated because of his failure to build a relationship with David (see 1 Sam. 25). Abigail knew how to appeal to David to
accomplish her goal; she assumed a servant role, feeling secure enough
to serve; she gave David and his army what they needed; and she added
value to David and saved the life of her family.[12]

While no one style or theory of leadership described above is intrin-
sically better than another, just considering them calls attention to the
wide range of behaviors available to leaders. And they may provide us a
bridge toward building consensus.

Consensus Building

Consensus building is also known as collaborative problem solving. It is
based on the ideas of participation and ownership of decisions. It attempts
to include all those charged with making a decision. All the participants
have the opportunity to voice their opinions, relevant ideas about a particular problem are presented, power is equalized, and a unanimous agreement is reached. The agreement is based on compromise or on the ability
of the group to find common ground for concurrence. It is often time
consuming, but it is better than blithely favoring the status quo.

Consensus building is often employed to settle multiparty issues,
conflicts, and disputes. Heidi Burgess and Brad Spangler, of Leadership
Strategies, Inc., have determined that people tend to disagree for one of
three reasons: they have not clearly heard and understood the other's
alternative and reasons for supporting the alternative; they have heard
and understood, but they have had different experiences or hold different values that result in preferring one alternative to the other; or the
disagreement is based on personality, past history with one another, or
other factors that have nothing to do with the alternatives.[13] In most cases
the reason is the first one.

Consensus has the power to change things or to prevent those changes
if they are unacceptable to all entities. According to Burgess and Spangler,
a number of problems in the work on consensus building have been identified: Perhaps problems are not well defined, or there is disagreement
about how they should be defined, or several participants have a vested

interest in the problems and are interdependent. There may be a disparity of power and/or resources for dealing with the problems among the participants. The problems may be characterized by technical complexity and scientific uncertainty. In addition, differing perspectives on the problems often lead to adversarial relationships among the participants. Incremental or unilateral efforts to deal with the problems typically produce less than satisfactory solutions. Plus, existing processes for addressing the problems have proved insufficient and may even exacerbate them.

Any number of guidelines could be presented as solutions for building consensus. One of those procedures is to trust one another. Everyone should be involved, and each person is free to express an idea or opinion. Those ideas or opinions should be presented clearly and logically. In addition, everyone must understand the problem and stay on task. The issue should be separated from the personalities involved. A decision should not be reached just to avoid conflict. It should not be based on a majority vote or on averages. Bargaining should be avoided. Minds should be engaged in the decision-making process. Approval of a decision should be reached, and the decision should be implemented.

The American Youth Foundation originally designed what they called the "fist-to-five" approach to building consensus.[14] They suggested the technique of determining what each person's opinion is at any given time. The leader restates a decision that has been made and asks everyone to show their level of support. Each participant responds by showing a fist or a number of fingers that represents their opinion. A fist represents a no vote and blocks consensus. The person showing a fist is saying that they want to talk more about the problem or require changes be made in the decision for it to pass. One finger indicates a need to discuss certain issues and suggest changes that should be made. Two fingers means the person is comfortable with the decision but would like to discuss some minor issues. Three fingers indicate a lack of total agreement, but the person is comfortable enough to let the decision pass without further discussion. Four fingers designate it's a good decision and a willingness to work on it. Five fingers indicate it's a great decision and a willingness to lead in its implementation.

This model recommends that if anyone holds up fewer than three fingers, they should be given the opportunity to state their objections and that person's concerns should be addressed. The "fist-to-five" process will be continued until consensus has been reached; that is, until a minimum of three fingers is showing on every participant's hand. Only then can the team move on to the next problem or issue.

Four primary determinants of a successful consensus process have been identified by Burgess and Spangler. First, the participants must be interdependent so that none of them can achieve on their own what the group will be able to achieve through collaboration. Second, participants must deal with their differences in a constructive way. Third, there must be joint or group ownership of the decisions made. Fourth, consensus building must be an emergent process, so decisions must be carried out in a flexible way.[15]

The ability to help groups work together to create solutions to a problem and reach decisions is a skill that can be developed. According to Michael Wilkinson, certified master facilitator and author, there are five techniques for building consensus: delineate alternatives, discuss strengths and weaknesses, merge alternatives, build criteria lists and score alternatives, and converge upon an alternative.[16] Although the starting point may appear to be significant because of the disagreement or conflict, a skillful leader can get the group to "yes."

You can create value; you can allocate all the gains available to those with whom you are working. The optimistic leader believes value can be created in spite of any differences in issues or values of the group. The skills you garner over time to build community, achieve collaboration, and develop consensus will allow you and everyone with whom you work to grow successful, to get everything they want out of the process. And it will increase your longevity multifold.

Reality Check (Q/A)

1. In your opinion, is the building of a human community of positive and spiritual relations on an uphill or downhill slope? Why?

2. Why do you think community building is a process of constructing unselfish relationships among people around a
   common interest?

3. What are the four stages of community building according to M.
   Scott Peck? Explain each stage.

4. What are the general characteristics of "community people,"
   according to Jerry L. Hampton? Do you agree? Why?

5. What is your definition of "collaboration"?

6. In your opinion, what are the top five successful collaboration
   components? Compare your list with other learners. How do
   they differ?

7. Do you agree or disagree that if a team collaborates internally
   they will be able to compete externally? Why?

8. What are some of the advantages of collaborative efforts
   at work?

9. Do you agree or disagree that collaborative efforts succeed
   where traditional leadership methods fail? Why?

10. What are the six traditional leadership theories? Which one
    appeals to you the most? Why?

11. In your opinion, what is the purpose of collaborative problem
    solving and consensus building?

12. What are some guidelines for building consensus toward
    a solution?

13. What is your personal opinion of the "fist-to-five" consensus
    building technique?

14. What are the primary determinants of a successful consensus
    building process?

15. Do you believe with optimistic leaders that value can be created
    in spite of any differences in issues or values of a group? Explain.

Case Study: Collaboration and Consensus Building

For the past fourteen years, the Promenade Avenue Church, located in a
mid-sized city, has maintained a grassroots' collaboration with the nearby

Prairie Hills Elementary School. The school struggles to provide the necessary resources to students, the majority of them living in poverty. Oscar is a deacon of the church and oversees the church's outreach ministry. He proposes to the elders that the church engage in a collaborative effort with the school. When he is asked whether or not the church should be involved with student academics rather than with teaching them about Christ, Oscar argues, "We are in a relationship with the school both by our physical proximity and by our calling as the body of Christ. Our mission is not to save the school but to love and care for its students and their parents, improve the students' lives, and revive the neighborhood. This is a very tangible way in which we can follow Jesus' teaching and be a light to our world."

After the elders approved the ministry, Oscar went and talked to Ms. Gulliver, the principal of Prairie Hills, to see if they would want the church's help, and if so, what specific aids she thought her students might need to become more successful students. Ms. Gulliver did want the church's help and identified the most pressing need as improved writing skills of their second-graders. So Oscar appealed to several church members to volunteer their time to help second-graders with writing the alphabet. He talked to those who showed an interest in the program and inquired what talents and abilities they thought they had that could be used to help students. Once he got four volunteers, they began meeting with second-graders selected by teachers and the principal, got parent permission to tutor them after school, and began helping the students.

After three years, the school saw a marked increase in students' ability to write and spell. Ms. Gulliver and several teachers also started to see a decrease in social unrest and fights between students. The principal also got reports that families were formally requesting that their children remain at the school even after the family has moved outside the school's boundaries. Student achievement was becoming exceptionally strong for a high-poverty school. Despite high poverty in families, student academic achievement was stronger and mobility rates were lower, thereby defying two demographic factors proven to affect student achievement: poverty and high mobility.

The relationship between the school and church evolved over the next several years to include more volunteers and more services for students. What began as a relationship-based, letter-writing initiative in second grade expanded exponentially to include a focus on reading, tutoring, and mentoring, as well as enrichment activities not previously available at the school or in the community. Every student in grades two through four had a family from the congregation who sponsored that child. Over the years other programs emerged as members of the congregation saw needs they could meet. Oscar involved a team of church members to organize and maintain a funded after-school arts enrichment program, a children's choir, a summer soccer league, tutoring, classroom assistance, donations of all kinds, grade-level field trips, holiday parties and birthday celebrations, neighborhood housing and beautification efforts, school facility beautification, and individual and church support of children, families, and school staff in crisis.

After just four years of this program, the school-church collaboration is lauded as successful throughout the community and has achieved statewide recognition for student academic achievement and volunteer commitment.

1. What actions did Oscar likely take that would have helped him elicit volunteers and mobilize them into action?
2. What key ingredients are likely to have contributed to the success of this program, via the interaction and discourse of Oscar, the elders, the principal, the teachers, the parents, and the volunteers?
3. What role does consensus building play in the collaborative effort of the church and school?

Notes

[1] C.S. Lewis, *Mere Christianity*, rev. ed. (San Francisco: HarperCollins, 2001), 134-135.

[2] M. Scott Peck, *The Different Drum: Community Making and Peace* (New York: Touchstone, 2010).

[3] Jerry L. Hampton, "Exploration into Personal Interspace" in *The Fire of Large Groups* (Stuttgart: Klett-Cotta: 2005), Accessed on July 31 2015, http://www.community4me.com/communitybldg1.html.

[4] Paul W. Mattessich, Marta Murray-Close, and Barbara R. Monsey, *Collaboration: What Makes It Work: A Review of Research Literature on Factors Influencing Successful Collaboration* (Amherst H. Wilder Foundation: 1992), 7.

[5] Douglas B. Richardson, "Think and Do: The Battle between Autonomy and Collaboration," *Edge International Journal* (May 2013): 56-61.

[6] David D. Chrislip and Carl E. Larson, *Collaborative Leadership: How Citizens and Civic Leaders Can Make a Difference* (San Francisco: Jossey-Bass, 1994).

[7] Edwin P. Hollander, *Leadership Dynamics* (University of California: Free Press, 1984).

[8] Fred E. Fiedler, *A Theory of Leadership Effectiveness* (McGraw Hill, 1967).

[9] James M. Kouzes and Barry Z. Bozeman, *The Leadership Challenge* (San Francisco: Jossey-Bass, 2008).

[10] Robert J. House, "A 1976 Theory of Charismatic Leadership," in James G. Hunt & Lars.L. Larson (Eds.), *Leadership: The Cutting Edge* (Carbondale: Southern Illinois University Press, 1977), 331.

[11] John C. Maxwell, *The Maxwell Bible: Lesson in Leadership from the Word of God* (Nashville, TN: Thomas Nelson, 2003), 1344.

[12] Maxwell Bible, 359-360.

[13] Heidi Burgess and Brad Spangler, "Consensus Building," Beyond Intractability, Conflict Research Consortium, University of Colorado, September 2003, http://www.beyondintractability.org/essay/consensus-building/.

[14] Adam Fletcher, Firestarter Participant Guidebook (Olympia, Washington: The Freechild Project, 2002).

[15] Burgess and Spangler, http://www.beyondintractability.org/essay/consensus-building/.

[16] Michael Wilkinson, "Building Consensus: The Art of Getting to Yes: Five Techniques for Building Consensus," Leadership Strategies (Blog), Accessed July 11, 2015, http://www.leadstrat.com/blog/the-art-of-getting-to-yes-5-techniques-for-building-consensus-2/.

CHAPTER 12

Communicate Responsibly

His sheep follow him because they know his voice.

John 10:4

Most of us are recognized by our voices. Even before the days of Caller ID, when a friend or family member called and you heard their voice, you knew in an instant who was speaking. Our voices are unique. They express our identity. There may be occasions when two people (members of the same family) sound similar, but when their voices are listened to carefully, distinctions in tone and articulation can be detected. Like an oral fingerprint, our voices help to identify us.

Our voices not only help to identify *who* we are, but *how* we are. If we are feeling sad or depressed, the tone of our voice can give it away. If we are excited or apprehensive, this too can come across by the pace and pitch of our voices. People can use their voices to let others know when they are feeling angry, scared, joyful, and apprehensive—whatever our mood may be.

Professionals will train their voices so as to make the most connection or impact on those who hear them. Whether we are talking about a newscaster's articulation of the news, a politician's speeches to roomfuls of potential voters and supporters, or a music performer who wants to capture the range of pitches their voice can make in order to create a distinctive sound, understanding how the voice can be used to communicate is vitally important. Business leaders know that effective communication is more than becoming an expert in communication technology. In an article in *The Harvard Business Review,* JoJo Tabres reports that in a survey *Review* readers ranked communication skills as more important than ambition, education, and willingness to work.[1] Communication is an extremely important skill for anyone wishing to be a manager or a good spouse, or for someone who wishes to acquire wealth.

This is also true of good leaders. The voice of a good leader communicates his or her wisdom, power, and authority to lead others. When Jesus said that "sheep" (people who belong to God's spiritual flock) hear the voice of the Good Shepherd (Jesus), he meant that they know from his voice that he is the one with authority and wisdom to lead them to be fed and protected. They trust him and his "voice" (his manner of communicating with them) is so detectable that they will not be fooled by imitators or imposters.

Like a good shepherd, longtime leaders know there is a balanced voice critical to use when communicating responsibly. Whether they are conscious of them or not, longtime leaders know several crucial elements of effective communication. Getting it right ensures their followers and employees that they are wise enough, compassionate enough, and focused enough to lead them where they need to go. In this chapter, we will explore six ways of communicating that appear to make a tremendous difference in whether or not a person will lead others for a long time. What is crucial, however, is that these items be balanced in order to create the responsible voice for longtime leadership. If the qualities are not balanced, leaders could mistakenly impact their organizations in a direction that would be detrimental to their effectiveness.

Communicate Positively but Not Disingenuously

One of the most positive communicators in the last several years undoubtedly is Dr. Randy Pausch. Pausch was Associate Professor of Computer Science at Carnegie Mellon University when he discovered at the age of forty-six that he had pancreatic cancer. He underwent surgery and chemotherapy, but they did not halt the progression of the disease. During this period of treatment Pausch was given the grim news that he would not have long to live. So, with the assistance of Jeffrey Zaslow, a reporter with the *Wall Street Journal,* Pausch wrote *The Last Lecture.*[2] The book is a revision of several lectures he gave at CMU. The University asks its leading academics to guide students to think more deeply about what is important in life by giving a lecture as if it were their last one. Pausch had given several of these. They were combined in this popular book.

Pausch's book became a *New York Times* bestseller, and his resulting lecture became a national phenomenon. Millions of people watched his talk on YouTube, and Pausch was even invited to give a mini-version of it on the Oprah Winfrey Show. The notoriety of his lecture came about in part, not only because of his fight with cancer and the truthfulness of the points he makes, but because Pausch himself communicated his wisdom and insight positively and with humor. He focused on what is true in the world, what is good, what is pleasant, and what would bring hope and inspiration to others.

Are you a positive communicator? Are you someone who points out what is going well, what is excelling, what is edifying and encouraging? It is easy to be the naysayer, always pointing out what is wrong, what is not working, what has failed, and what is disappointing. But does simply pointing out the negative or mistakes in things and in others really inspire people to follow you?

Positive communicators use their voices to project a positive attitude. They are optimistic and are confident that hurdles can be overcome. They see new challenges as opportunities to exercise or to gain new skills or to experience new growth.

But communicating positively requires balance. Some people think that communicating positive messages is so important that it is justifiable to stretch the truth. Speaking positively, however, does not mean one has to be disingenuous. Some people in positions of leadership do not make this distinction. They know that it is important to be seen as positive, so they are willing to distort or conceal negative information in order to keep a positive spin on what is actually a bad situation. Sometimes these irresponsible individuals are easy to spot. You see them talking about how everything is going great and what a wonderful future the company or church has, when everyone in the organization knows all too well that things are not great and that serious issues exist that must be addressed and solved.

This type of glib, saccharine positivity is not what is meant by communicating positively. People see through the charade. When leaders attempt to fake optimism, followers will detect that someone is trying to pull the wool over their eyes merely to stay positive. They then lose respect for said leader and will be reluctant to follow them.

An additional negative impact of such disingenuousness as fake optimism is that it stops conversation and discussions about how to solve problems. People in organizations and institutions do not want to fail. They want to help correct problems and share the load of responsibility to get systems working more effectively. But when leaders try to deceive them with a false positivity, people feel disrespected and distrusted. They begin to doubt that leadership really does want them involved in solving the problems. People then do not initiate conversations with leadership to overcome challenges. Instead they wait to see what solutions the leaders will come up with themselves.

On the other hand, leaders who experience a long tenure communicate a positive vision and accentuate the positive aspects of the organization, but they know that to conceal unpleasant news or information erodes trust and weakens their ability to lead. Speaking positively about what an organization can achieve is balanced with speaking honestly about what is wrong and what needs to be fixed to move the organization forward.

Communicate Passionately but Not Theatrically

Billy Graham will long be remembered as one of the great evangelists of the twentieth century. He will not be remembered because of any particular phrase such as Martin Luther King's "I have a dream" speech. What he will be remembered for most of all is the passion with which he communicated his sermons. Graham preached with such intensity because he was convinced that there were people in his audience who would be lost for eternity if they did not repent of their sins and place their whole trust in Jesus Christ as their personal Savior. Thousands upon thousands would cram large stadiums to hear Graham preach a message that many had heard preached before: believe in Jesus as the Son of God and you will be saved. What Graham was preaching wasn't novel, but how he preached it was captivating. His passionate preaching was a key element in his ability to persuade his audience not only to trust his message but also to trust him. Passion very often communicates sincerity and authenticity.

Leaders who lead for a long time know that they need to be trusted by those who follow them. Of course, their followers will want to know that what their leader has to say is accurate and well-informed, but if they are going to exert energy and effort in following that leader, they want to know that the leader is personally committed. The leader communicates by speaking words with unabashed passion.

Communicating passionately doesn't mean communicating theatrically. Some leaders are so eager to be heard that they are more focused on the form of what they say than on the content of it. A leader who wants to "put on a show" or "make a big splash" can certainly get someone's attention. But these attention-getters are hardly the long-term leaders of effective, successful companies. Very soon followers can perceive the difference between a leader who can communicate their vision and direction with passion and one who simply wants to be heard or to make a grand appearance. Leaders with longevity are passionate communicators who do not fall into the trap of thinking that in order to be heard and followed they have to be showy or visually spectacular. The soundness of a clearly stated vision communicated by the honest passion of the leader is the balance that compels others to follow for the long term.

Communicate Confidently but Not Arrogantly

Speaking confidently is a huge asset if a person wants to inspire trust from others. People seldom trust someone who lacks confidence either in themselves or in the organization they intend to lead. Unfortunately, some leaders are confident about their own ability to lead but fail to speak in such a manner that their confidence is perceived by others. They speak in hesitant language that makes them sound uncertain about what can be done ("Well, maybe," "I'll try," "I hope I can," etc.). And in many circumstances, what those who are meant to follow hear or see in their leader is not confidence but arrogance. The leader irresponsibly talks incessantly about their own strengths, abilities, and experience, as if they have to convince others that they are fortunate to have them as their leader. Arrogance can easily be detected and only persuades would-be followers to be cautious about trusting such would-be leaders.

So how does a confident leader responsibly communicate confidently while avoiding the trap of speaking arrogantly? A lot of advice has been offered about how a person can sound and look confident when speaking. Many communication experts prescribe that communicators should stand up straight but relaxed, make good eye-contact, breathe smoothly, etc. But communicating confidently is fundamentally rooted in healthy self-confidence, and it can be detected even when perfect eye-contact and breathing techniques are absent.

A leader who speaks confidently will sound authentic. Not everyone who does speak "straight from the heart" will be perceived as doing so. But those who are perceived as confident are also seen as speaking genuinely about their values and beliefs. What confident-sounding leaders say will come across as rising out of their deep convictions about what is the right direction to go and what needs to be done to get to the goal.

Confident sounding leaders also often speak with humor, especially self-deprecating humor. These leaders are not afraid to laugh with others, or even to have, on occasions, their own mistakes laughed at by followers. Despite making some errors in judgments, they are humble enough and confident enough that they still have the vision and ability to take their organization into new directions.

Finally, leaders who speak confidently but not arrogantly are those who realize how indebted they are to those who follow them. They express gratitude for the contribution and difference others make in the organization. Longtime leaders often are heard enthusiastically thanking others about specific things people are doing that are making a difference. What we are describing here is not the glib, generic "thanks" that shows no indication that the leader personally knows the effort or merit of the work done. Effective expressions of thanks contain concrete reference to the particulars of the contribution that has been made. Sounding confident is not at odds with showing indebtedness to others. In fact, the reverse is characteristic of confident-sounding leaders. They are genuinely and authentically grateful for those around them and are not hesitant to vocalize that appreciation frequently.

Communicate Clearly but Not Patronizingly

Our word *simple* is actually complicated. Depending upon the context in which it is used, like most words it can convey different ideas. For instance, it is commonly used to describe something as being easy or uncomplicated to perform, such as when someone might say, "This is a simple plan." But it is also used to point out something as "honest," such as in the sentence, "I just want the simple truth." Sometimes the word is used positively, and sometimes it is used to characterize things negatively. If a person says of another person, "She lives a simple life," that may be a compliment noting that the person is not entangled with a lot of material goods. But if a person says of another person, "He is simple," the intent may be to characterize that individual as unintelligent or naïve.

It is this negative usage of the word that critics of communicators have in mind when they deride great speeches as "simple." A "simple speech" is criticized for having content and/or delivery of a message that lacks ideological sophistication, depth, and comprehensiveness. But what these critics miss is that outstanding communicators know ideas and visions are often best communicated with simple clarity. This does not mean that a clear communicator is a "simple" person or that their ideas are "simple." But what many effective leaders do realize is that in order to convey one's ideas or thoughts to others, people need to visualize clearly and simply what you want them to know. They want you to paint a clear word picture, much like a cartoonist captures the essence with a few strokes of a pen.

We teach at a university where its faculty, even the tenured faculty, are regularly evaluated by their students. One of the comments I occasionally get from some of my students is, "Professor Harrison uses big words." This remark is not intended as a compliment! What the students are expressing is that sometimes in class I will use terms or expressions that are unique within my discipline of New Testament studies but are unclear in meaning to the general public. I take this criticism seriously. While I certainly know that in a university setting professors are supposed to introduce students to new vocabulary, it is also vitally important for professors to communicate clearly with their students. If I use technical jargon and assume students will either know it or will take the time to look up its definition, I am unclear to those I am entrusted to instruct.

But communicating clearly should not be confused with speaking patronizingly. A person intent on being clear does not have to resort to language which might give the impression that they are talking down to others. Leaders who address their audience condescendingly or patronizingly sound like they believe others are unintelligent or too dense to comprehend complex problems. These irresponsible leaders treat followers as if they were small children by prefacing their remarks with statements such as, "Now let me see if I can help you understand this," or "I'll try to put this in simple terms for you." Comments that are aimed at belittling followers' capabilities to comprehend information only irritate them and erode trust.

Unwise leaders use patronizing and condescending language in order to remind followers that they do not have the ability to tackle the complexity of leadership that they themselves do. Such language is aimed at maintaining the status of the leader as superior both in intellect and wisdom. However, the irony is that such language actually ends up eliminating any respect the leader might have had. Longtime leaders know that people usually trust those who trust them. It is difficult for followers to believe that their leader trusts them when she or he addresses them with a condescending, superior attitude. Leaders who communicate responsibly can be clear about what followers need to know and still address them as intelligent, insightful individuals worthy of total respect.

Communicate Repeatedly but Not Repetitively

The old adage "Communicate, Communicate, Communicate" is still true if a person or an organization wants to communicate effectively. It highlights the truth that within groups and organizations, people need to be reminded often of what is important or why they need to know the information. Productive, longtime leaders comprehend the value of repeating what they want those they lead to know and do.

These leaders realize that followers are bombarded with so much information on a daily basis and often with a lot of misinformation about what is going on "behind the scene." So it is crucial for leadership to repeat the essential message they want others to understand. If followers only hear information once or twice, it is easy for them to mis-hear what was said. But when leaders repeat information several times on different occasions, this can go a long way toward increasing clarity and understanding and toward minimizing misinterpretion of the speaker.

There is a danger. If the one communicating only repeats the exact same information in the exact same tone and by the exact same method, then they are not only repeating themselves. They risk being irresponsibly boring and repetitive. Now you might be asking, "Well, aren't 'repeating' and 'repetitive' describing the same thing?" Well, no, not in the way we are using them here. There is a difference. Knowing the difference is what distinguishes the responsibly communicating longtime leaders from the rest of the pack.

A repetitive communicator fails to grasp the monotonous impact of a message that has no variety in the way it is presented. Listeners who get the same information delivered to them in precisely the same way may end up believing that what they are actually getting is the "company line" rather than what is really important to the leader. A leader who presents over and over again the same tired line will appear rigid and out of touch, while one who reinvents the way crucial information is disseminated moves their organization toward greater clarity and trust.

Communicate Praise but Not Flattery

By its very definition flattery is thought of as manipulative while praise is primarily perceived as a positive, if not at times a necessary, form of communication. Scripture is replete with exhortations to praise God (Ps. 150; Matt. 5:16; Rev. 19:15) and to verbally honor others (Ex. 20:12; Rom. 12:10; 1 Pet. 2:17). However, the Bible never condones flattery. Instead the Scriptures give us warnings about those who with lying tongues deceitfully attempt to win their way through words (Prov. 12:2; 26:28; Rom. 16:18).

There are people who are fully aware that what most people want is to be respected and appreciated. Knowing this, they seek to gain trust by playing to people's hunger to be significant. After several occasions of being manipulated by flattery, most victims of this deception wise up and realize that flatterers are not to be trusted for their words that just sound like praise. Flatterers might experience a short run of gaining the appreciation, respect, and admiration of others, but such individuals are not the examples of longtime leaders who contribute to the good of their organization.

Praising, on the other hand, is something longtime leaders are known to do well. Praise arises out of sincere appreciation for the accomplishment of others. A leader who praises knows what a flatterer knows, namely, that people want and need to be recognized for their achievements. The difference, however, is that a leader who praises followers does so not with the intent of rising in their estimation of himself/herself, but rather because they know that genuine praise creates a positive emotional experience that often will inspire and rejuvenate the one who is praised. Because the leader wants competent, accomplished followers to feel energized from such communication, they are never hesitant to praise those whose work and effort have earned it.

Your Personal Conversational Archetype

In the next chapter, we will be looking at listening and its importance. Before that, what is your personal conversational archetype (your model or prototype). Randy Pausch offers six possibilities by which you can identify yourself.

1. *The Pretender.* "You'd swear he was hanging on every word you uttered, and you'd walk out of his office feeling like a million bucks, won over completely by his knowing, empathetic smile." Then nothing you talked about would ever actually happen.

2. *The Opinionator.* "One CEO of a major company, a seasoned executive, had a habit of cutting people off three sentences into the presentation of a new idea. 'Look,' he would snap, 'let me tell you how I see this. . . . ' From there, he would proceed to express his opinion with no uncertainty."

3. *The Grouch.* "Whereas the Opinionator's listening is limited by his belief that his ideas are right, the Grouch is blocked by the certainty that your ideas are wrong."

4. *The Preambler.* "Television pundits have become the very embodiment of the poor-listening archetype, the Preambler, whose windy lead-ins and questions are really stealth speeches."

5. *The Perseverator.* "The Perseverator may appear to be engaged in productive dialogue, but if you pay attention, you might notice that he's not really advancing the conversation."

6. *The Answer Man.* "This is the person who starts spouting solutions before there is even a consensus about what the challenge might be, signaling that he is finished listening to your input in the conversation."[3]

In all honesty, you are probably a mixture of all six archetypes. It may depend on the circumstances. Or perhaps when you are faced with a difficult question, you choose to answer an easier question. The result is a compounding of the communication process.

John Mackey, cofounder and co-CEO of Whole Foods, on Inc.com suggests that articulation (enunciation, speech, delivery) is overrated. You also might have got that idea when you were reading descriptions of the archetypes above. "Back then I was more impressed with people who were very articulate...," Mackey admits, "I got snowed by a few of those people over the years." He says he now values character first—"someone who is hardworking, candid, and ambitious, while still showing humility"—when he tries to identify future leaders.[4]

He says, "I also look for people who have a high degree of emotional intelligence—a high capacity for caring. I think for leadership positions, emotional intelligence is more important than cognitive intelligence. People with emotional intelligence usually have a lot of cognitive intelligence, but that's not always true the other way around."

Is Mackey talking about you? We know many people who are never at a loss for confidence when they speak to individuals, small groups, or large audiences. At the same time, we know others who are so fearful that they are embarrassed to speak in public, some who won't lead a prayer in Sunday School or at a small dinner (even in their own home if guests are there). And then there are those who would claim to be born introverts but often stand in front of a roomful of people to speak, coach, conduct a workshop, deliver a sermon, or sell something.

Doug Conant, the former Campbell Soup CEO, says he uses his shyness to forge close relationships and build trust with people. His advice?

- *Don't change who you are.* All introverts aspire to be more outgoing, but it's not in our nature. I discovered that the best thing to do was to tell everyone I worked with that I'm just shy. People are not mind readers—you need to let them know. It builds a strong sense of trust and gets beyond all of the little superficial dances people do.
- *Say what's on your mind.* Some jobs are emotionally challenging, but you have to get the job done. Telling your colleagues something that is on your mind is so much easier than keeping it in. Sometimes the things we make up in our heads are not nearly as big a deal as we think.
- *Know who you work with.* Most people think of leaders as being these outgoing, very visible, and charismatic people, which I find to be a very narrow perception. The key challenge is to get beyond the surface of your colleagues. You might just find that

you have introverts embedded within your organization who are natural-born leaders. Extroverts may get places faster, but for introverts it's all about working at the pace you need and, at the end of the day, performing at your best.

- *Find alone time.* Introverts get more energy by having quiet time, compared with extroverts, who find energy by being around people.[5]

Whether an introvert, an extrovert, or somewhere in between, you can be the person who communicates your messages with success. The guidelines in this chapter should help you overcome any perceived awkwardness in sharing your messages, feelings, or thoughts. You can have the voice of a balanced long-term leader.

Reality Check (Q/A)

1. How do our voices help to identify who we are and how we are?
2. How does the voice of a good leader communicate his or her wisdom, power, and authority to others?
3. What are the six ways of communicating that appear to make a tremendous difference in whether or not a person will lead others for a long time? Give an example of each.
4. How do you personally communicate positively but not disingenuously? Passionately but not theatrically? Confidently but not arrogantly? Clearly but not patronizingly? Repeatedly but not repetitively? Praise but not flattery?
5. Who are some longtime leaders who demonstrate each of the ways of communicating in question four?
6. What are the six possibilities by which you can identify your personal conversational archetype? Give an example of each.
7. Of the six possibilities in question six, which one is most like you? Explain.
8. Do you know someone who seems never at a loss for confidence when asked to speak to individuals, small groups, or large audiences? Describe that person.

9. How might you use shyness to forge close relationships and build trust with people?

10. What are some perceived awkwardnesses you have discovered in yourself? Explain.

Case Study: Communication

Ken Boatright had been an associate minister at the Newton Avenue Church for two years before he and two other staff members were laid off because of the economic recession. His senior minister, Larry Gardner, apologized profusely for having to take this drastic action. Ken decided to meet with the senior minister at another church in that state for a possible position he thought they had been advertising. Unfortunately, they were affected by the same recession problems and were having to cut their budget back and not hire anyone. Ken was disappointed, but eventually he found an even better employment opportunity out of state, took the job, and moved.

After one year in his new position, Ken, always a researcher at heart, wrote a journal article for a brotherhood publication. It was published after nine months in another person's book of readings about congregational leadership. Ken received several copies of the book from the publisher. He wanted to share this book with his former boss at Newton Avenue and called the senior minister to tell him about the book. Unfortunately the telephone call with Diana, a new secretary to the church and someone who had just recently moved into the community, did not go well.

Diana: "Newton Avenue Church. How may I help you?"

Ken: "I'd like to speak with Larry Gardner, please, if he is available."

Diana: "What do you want?" she said sarcastically. "We don't have any employment opportunities, so there's no need for you to talk to him."

Ken. "I'm not calling about an employment opportunity. You shouldn't assume that people only call for employment opportunities. I want to send him a complimentary copy of a book which has an article in it that I wrote. The senior minister knows me and will be glad to share my success."

Diana: "No. No. No. The senior minister sees everything and knows everything. Every article published is known to him. You'd just be wasting his time mailing him another book."

Ken: "It's not just any book. It's published by a globally prestigious publisher, and I want to personally inform him about it by gifting him the book."

Diana: "I can't let you talk to him. He's too busy to deal with such."

Ken: "Okay, I'll just mail him the book and email him about it."

Diana: "All right." (She said impolitely.) "Goodbye."

Ken hung up the phone, contemplating what had just happened. He mailed the book unenthusiastically and emailed his former boss. He decided not to say anything about his conversational gambit with the new secretary.

A week later Ken received an email from his ex-boss congratulating him for the publication and thanking him for the book. Ken felt excited that his ex-employer was pleased about the book and was looking forward to reading it.

1. What are the communication challenges above?
2. Was Diana right to discourage Ken from speaking to the senior minister or mailing a copy of the book?
3. Did Diana empathize with Ken? Explain.
4. What were some of the challenges that prevented smooth communication between Ken and Diana?
5. What prevented Diana from displaying courteous listening skills and made her draw the conclusions or preconceived notions she acted on?
6. Should Ken have told Larry about the incident? Why?
7. What actions would you recommend that Ken take if he should encounter a similar incident again?

Notes

[1] JoJo Tabares, "Communication Technology Doesn't Replace Communication Skills!" http://creation.com/communication-technology-doesnt-replace-communication-skill/.

[2] Randy Pausch with Jeffrey Zaslow, *The Last Lecture*: The Legacy Edition (Hyperion Books: 2008).

[3] Bernard T. Ferrari, *Power Listening: Mastering the Most Critical Business Skill of All* (New York: Penguin, 2012).

[4] Inc Magazine, "John Mackey of Whole Foods on Hiring Leaders," July 1, 2009, http://www.inc.com/magazine/20090701/john-mackey-of-whole-foods-on-hiring-leaders.html/.

[5] Caitlin Keating, "How Introverts Can be Leaders," *Fortune* (May 21, 2012), 56.

CHAPTER 13

Be an Engaged Listener

My dear brothers, take note of this: Everyone should be quick to listen,
slow to speak and slow to become angry.

James 1:19

Unless you've been living in a cave or confined to a lonely cubicle offline, you know the importance of contact with others. Leaders in churches or businesses know the importance of being articulate and benefiting from full communication with those they come in contact with. This implies successful receipt of a message as well as the competence to send one. Listening, therefore, is a critical skill. Of all the available sources of information in order for leaders to accurately assess the personalities of those around them, listening is the most important. It is a crucial part of leading others for a long time.

Research indicates that, unfortunately, normal listening patterns result in only a 50 percent retention immediately after a ten-minute presentation, with a decline to 25 percent after two months. The average person experiences a 75 percent information loss because of poor listening skills.

Because of this incredible statistic, leaders face a critical problem not only in getting messages through but also in receiving messages.

One reason for such discouraging listening-retention rates is the mind's ability to think four-to-six times faster than the average person speaks (600–800 words per minute thinking speed versus 125–150 words per minute speaking). The listener finds it easy to tune in and out or to take side thought trips while the speaker is transmitting a message at this relatively slower speed. Consequently, the listener often indulges in a type of hop-skip-jump listening pattern, pretending to pay attention but actually yielding to distractions rather than comprehending what is said.

This chapter will explore the reasons why listening is such an important contributing factor to the longevity of leaders.

You Can't Listen in One Minute!

In his best-selling book *The One Minute Manager,* Kenneth Blanchard popularized the vision of efficiency in management by portraying a fictional executive who had a great reputation as a productive manager.[1] The hero-manager of the story trusts those he has delegated certain tasks to and does not spend a large amount of his time analyzing how every step of the task is being carried out. Instead, this executive spends only a few minutes each week with each project supervisor to give them brief positive feedback for tasks that are being completed accurately and on time. He offers brief corrective guidance when tasks were not being completed as expected.

The scenario Blanchard depicts is alluring, captivating, and filled with practical wisdom. But it would be a mistake to take Blanchard's image of the efficient manager and conclude that leadership of people can be done by spending little time listening to them. Longtime business and religious leaders know that in order to build trust, you have to spend time listening, and listening effectively.

We have to face the facts. Not everyone is predisposed to listen to what someone else says. In such cases, communication is not occurring, and chances are very good the job will not be carried out in accord with the expectations of the communicator. There may be several reasons why people don't listen or why conversation is not always communication. For example, in most day-to-day conversations between two individuals, each person's ego gets in the way of listening. As one person is speaking, the other person is thinking only of what to say when it is his or her turn to speak. What the average person listens for, in effect, is a moment of silence that will allow her or him to boost their ego by "taking the stage and holding forth."

Those Who Have Ears to Hear, Let Them Hear

There are times when the language or the terminology used turns off the listener because the words are emotionally charged. The emotions become so involved for or against the message that contact is lost with what is actually being said. Emotional deafness is the result. Thus the message received is seldom, if ever, the same as the message transmitted. The more involved people are in a particular situation, or with a problem, the less likely they are to listen objectively to what someone else is saying about it. The emotions of both sender and receiver affect their encoding and decoding of messages. To overcome this problem, leaders must prepare themselves mentally and emotionally to listen; they must try to develop a trusting relationship with the speaker. Better retention and higher levels of confidence in the message will be the result.

Mercifully, some people know instinctively how important it is to listen to others. In fact, listening comes to them naturally because they love being around people. They love social occasions when they can listen to what others have to say on a whole host of topics. Other leaders are more introverted. They accept the unavoidable reality that social occasions often come with the territory of leadership, but they are intimidated by such events. For these leaders, listening to people is an acquired taste.

Like many other acquired tastes, learning to value and enjoy the experience of listening to those you lead can be achieved. The pleasure of listening comes by understanding at a very personal level why listening is so important and experiencing the positive outcomes of practicing key listening skills. In the section that follows, we will highlight four interconnecting reasons that listening is so important, and we will consider what longtime leaders have come to understand about why listening is so significant.

Listening Is about Being Curious

Longtime leaders know that at the heart of listening is the desire to learn. A successful vice-president of an international shipping company was commenting on what makes the CEO of their company such an effective leader. He observed, "This guy is curious about everything that has to do with the business. From how the mail is handled to the challenges of shipping products to the interaction between staff and management, this CEO wants to learn and understand how our company operates at every level." What this CEO appreciates is that an important component of the learning process is discovering who does what and how it works every day in the organization. He knows that to thrive as a leader, he had to develop this crucial element of leadership: Listen to those you lead.

You've heard the old saying, "Curiosity killed the cat"? While there may be some truth to the notion that sticking one's nose in other people's business can do irreparable damage to relationships, constructive curiosity renews leaders. Constructive curiosity is different from the "cat-killing" kind. It is not about getting the latest gossip or satisfying a personal voyeurism into other people's lives. The curiosity that is constructive refuels commitments and recalls the purpose and aim of the organization. This curiosity builds healthier relationships in the process of discovering what contributes to a more effective organization.

Two key elements make leaders constructively curious. The first element is *intensity*. Constructive curiosity brings intensity to listening. Listening can be wearisome. Leaders, after all, have to receive a lot of information to make decisions. They hear from organizational "stockholders" who have deep personal investments (time, talents, finances, etc.) in the success and growth of the organization. They also hear from those over whom they are responsible, which in voluntary organizations can include "stockholders." (We're thinking here of church leaders who answer to congregational membership but also lead them.) Listening to a number of people from all over the organization can leave the leader feeling mentally, physically, and emotionally depleted. Over time, leaders might get to a stage where they think that they have heard and seen it all before. They might even conclude with the author of Ecclesiastes that "there is nothing new under the sun" (Eccl. 1:9).

When a leader reaches this moment, listening is experienced as routine and passionless. They already know all that they want to know, and they only go through the appearance of listening since their minds are already made up about what they will do. But if the leader maintains genuine curiosity, always wanting to learn and know more, realizing that no one but God has all the knowledge about all that can be known, then that leader will listen with an intensity that is transparent. People will sense that the leader is listening because he or she is sincerely interested in finding out all that can be learned from others that will make the group or the organization stronger, healthier, and more productive.

The second key element that is reflected in constructive curiosity is *humility.* Leaders who last listen to others curiously because they know that others may have ideas and perceptions that are better than their own. There is a difference between listening to others with interest because you know you don't have all the knowledge about all subjects and want to get additional information, and listening because you know that your knowledge about a particular subject might in fact be secondary to what others know about that subject. A leader who listens because they are genuinely inquisitive to know what will really help the organization is humble enough to listen to others by placing their own judgments and conclusions to the side while they investigate afresh the various perceptions others can bring. "Listening requires giving up our favorite human pastime—involvement in ourselves and our own self-interest."[2] Listening with genuine inquiry expresses humility. If leaders are arrogant or conceited, their listening will come across as distant and disconnected.

Listening Is Not Assuming

The second principle about listening that must be appreciated in order to become an effective longtime leader is to listen rather than to assume. It is a lot easier to simply assume you know why people behave the way they do instead of listening to their explanations as to why they take certain actions or believe specific things to be true. The Harvard Negotiation Project depicts a process by which someone can help mediate or negotiate all kinds of conflicts that occur at work and in our personal lives.[3] One piece of advice is that conflicts cannot be effectively resolved unless someone is taking the "Learning Stance." What is meant by this expression is that the person who is attempting to lead parties toward reconciliation, or at least toward understanding, has to determine what actually happened to cause the conflict. This means the person leading the reconciliation process must not assume (and must help the conflicted parties to not assume) that they know what happened and why. This process is described as disentangling a person's intent from the impact of their decision.

When leaders assume they know why others have acted the way they have, they often conclude that the person has improper intentions.[4] Leaders who assume that an employee or a member has acted improperly will frequently jump to this conclusion without ever truly listening to a person explain what they were thinking, feeling, and hoping at the time they made a decision that had a negative impact on the company or the church. What leaders need to apply in this situation is the Golden Rule: "Do to others what would have them do to you" (Matt. 7:12). Sadly, many leaders take the path of giving too many of those whom they lead less of the benefit of the doubt than they expect others to give to them. In other words, leaders who make mistakes hope the people they lead will trust that their leaders' intentions are to serve or provide the best for the companies they lead. But when one of the followers makes a mistake, what if the same graciousness that is desired by the leader is not offered to the follower? When leaders are repeatedly ungracious to those who make mistakes, they forfeit trust and are perceived as a liability to the organization.

An assumption is the first barrier leaders must avoid if they want to find common ground with their followers.[5] When we assume things about another person, we put them into a perceived "box." Once that is done, we no longer see the person as a true individual but, instead, as an example of a stereotype or generalization. Assuming is not only a barrier to finding common ground; it is also a barrier to the experience of listening. Rather than hearing what people actually have to say, we are listening for how people's words will confirm our assumptions about them. We think we have listened to them, but we are only listening to ourselves. Instead of assuming, longtime leaders listen to what their followers have to say.

Listening for Feelings and not Simply for Facts

Perceptive listeners, whether leaders or not, listen for more than the mere input of information. Certainly information is important. Leaders want to make the most informed decisions on the basis of the most accurate information. But information is hardly ever perceived as neutral, especially when such information is given to a leader with the expectation that she or he may act upon it. People feel things about information they share with decision makers. They may be enthusiastic about news that they think could greatly propel the organization (and possibly their own career) forward. They may be apprehensive about data that may require the company or the church to make fundamental changes about which goals to pursue and how. People who are giving information feel things about that information. They might feel angry, depressed, agitated, jubilant, defensive, vindicated, joyful, energized, hopeful, scared, appalled, agitated, or intrigued. Astute leaders will listen for the emotional tone with which the information is shared, and they will address the serious feelings along with the information.

One of the crucial feelings that long-lasting leaders are on the lookout for is anxiety. Anxiety, possibly more than any other emotion, can launch a person into a series of unproductive and destructive decisions or actions. There are four typical thought patterns of those who are anxious: false assumptions, catastrophic visions of the future, self-degradation, and mental criminalizing of others.[6]

What is so disabling about anxiety is that it restricts what a person can see as possible responses that can be taken in a given situation. Followers will not always tell a leader when they are feeling anxious about the organization. They may feel that revealing such information could be detrimental to their role or status in the group. This reluctance is why leaders who last must listen for feelings and not just for information.

Another reason why people will not often tell leaders how they feel about information is because putting feelings "out there" is risky. What happens if a person says to a leader, "Here is the information you wanted. Boy, if this stuff is accurate, I'm nervous!" A leader might dismiss such feelings as irrelevant to the task at hand. Feelings are not like other kinds of information. They are deeply personal. They are an extension of our identity and our worldview. For a leader to dismiss information from a follower as immaterial is one thing, but to discount how that follower feels is a bigger issue. No one wants to hear or sense that their feelings are silly, irrational, or inconsequential. For that reason, many followers never tell their leaders how they feel. They carefully disguise their feelings by the way they present information. Longtime leaders don't make the mistake of thinking that an organization can be run simply by making decisions on information and leaving feelings out of it. If the intense feelings of others are not acknowledged, affirmed, and addressed, they will often surface in negative ways throughout the organization.

However, before a leader can truly listen to the feelings of others, the leader needs to take ownership of how they feel when they hear other people express their feelings. What often happens among poor leaders is that they have not taken ownership of their own feelings and therefore are not prepared to respond responsibly to the feelings of others. If they sense that a person is angry or upset, they treat that emotion as a challenge to their leadership or authority. What they are failing to practice is a healthy detachment from the issue that may be upsetting the follower. This truth must be learned if a leader hopes to respond effectively to the emotions of church members. Church members regularly come to the senior minister, for example, with concerns about things they didn't like about the worship service or one of the ministries. Sometimes they express their concerns with a passionate intensity.

It is tempting to respond to these intense expressions of feelings defensively, assuming that their outrage means they dislike the senior minister personally. But some people express themselves passionately without intending to demean or to call into question those in charge. People have a right to have these feelings without having to conclude that the listener is the cause of them. Leaders who last for a long time know this truth well. When followers are annoyed or irritated, wise leaders do not jump to the conclusion that those feelings mean the upset person no longer respects them as good leaders. They have trained their emotional response to the unpleasant feelings of others in a way that shows they keep their personal identity detached from the organization and its issues and are therefore able to respond productively to the feelings of followers.

Listening Is the Art of Communicating Respect

Every leader knows that they cannot lead without the respect of their followers. But longtime leaders know that respect is a two-way street, and they must also respect those they lead. So how does respect relate to listening? When a leader listens, people feel respected, because the very act of listening sends additional messages which convey that the person speaking is valued. Some of these "messages" follow.

First, listening sends the message that you are worth valuable time. Time is a precious commodity to a leader. Wise ones know that they have to guard their time all the time so that they are investing their energy and attention on those things that make a difference for the organization, church, or group. When they use some of that precious time by intentionally giving it to listen to a follower, that act communicates respect. Moments like this are not the times that are spontaneously or haphazardly given to followers when they have cornered a leader in order to tell him or her what is on their mind. These moments are when leaders intentionally seek out followers and initiate a conversation with them because these followers want to know their leader and what their leader has to say.

A second message of respect communicated by listening is connectivity. When you genuinely listen to others, you are in essence saying, "I want to connect with you and the way you see things." This doesn't mean that leaders will always have to agree with the way followers see things, but it does mean that leaders are open to connecting to how others are seeing things. When you share with others your view of the world, your business, or your church, a connection is formed. This activity is certainly no easy task. There are as many different ways to look at the world as there are people on the planet. Listening to these various worldviews can be taxing and exhausting. It requires asking questions and gaining clarification. But the result of this effort to connect with others by listening to them demonstrates that they and their outlook on life or the organization are respected.

Finally, a third message of respect that is communicated when you listen is cooperation. When leaders listen to followers, they are implying that "we are in this together." The success of an organization never depends on one person or even on a few people; it depends on everyone doing their best in their responsibility. Everyone needs other people to help them succeed. No athlete, whether playing as an individual or on a team, reaches the championship alone. They have coaches, trainers, and people who support them emotionally, physically, and financially. No business makes it to the top simply because it has a highly qualified and competent CEO. It takes the efforts of multiple people to reach the corporate goal. Just being an articulate preacher doesn't make any church minister successful. It takes others working together, each carrying out their role, so that the church can function and build up each other (see Ephesians 4:1–11). When leaders take the time and make the connection with a follower to listen to what they have to say, they are showing by that act that they understand the person plays a role in the achievement and development of the group.

Not listening communicates disrespect. When followers sense that their input and judgment are never considered, they grow to distrust those who are in positions of leadership. They feel their opinions and insights are not valued, because they themselves are not valued. But when leaders listen to those who do the work or the ministry that propels the business or the church, they are communicating to those workers and volunteers that they are valued and that what they have to say about how things get done matters.

When Leaders Listen, People Speak

The popular E. F. Hutton commercials depicted a scene where two individuals are sitting in a crowded, noisy place. The two main characters are discussing some aspect of financial security in an economic climate of financial uncertainty. One of the characters says to the other, "Well, my investment counselor is with E. F. Hutton, and he says . . ." Then there is a distinct pause in the conversation, and the crowded area becomes eerily still. Not a single person makes a noise. Everyone's attention is on the actor who is about to tell his friend what E. F. Hutton says. The associated slogan that became famous with these ads told the viewers, "When E. F. Hutton speaks, people listen." The message is pretty clear. E. F. Hutton is knowledgeable about how the financial market works, so investors should be smart and listen to their advice.

It certainly is not true that everyone listens to E. F. Hutton. Investors have a wide range of knowledgeable and respected financial consultants to whom they can turn for advice. But it is true that when leaders truly listen to their followers, followers will speak to them. This is vitally important for leaders to understand. Leaders with longevity have learned the significance of having a reputation as a listener so others will speak. As mentioned earlier, leaders need to make decisions based on the best information they can get. But if a leader has a reputation of not listening to others, followers will purposely withhold information that could be valuable to the leader and the organization. When an organization has reached this stage, effective leadership and following cannot take place. If leaders wish to have their employees listen to what they say, they must first prove themselves to be persons who consistently listen with understanding. Those who are good listeners are usually repaid by having others listen to them, because listening is contagious.

Speak with Your Ears

On a visit to the University of Oklahoma, the renowned CBS news anchor Walter Cronkite said, "Eighty percent of communication is listening." His statistics may be an example of hyperbole, but the sentiment is certainly accurate. Leaders should do a lot more listening than talking. This truth is why the author of James told his audience to "be quick to listen," that is, be more eager to listen than to speak. Too often people foolishly assume that it is more important for others to listen to them than it is for them to listen to others. One of the lessons every executive seems to learn on the TV show "Undercover Boss" is the importance of listening to those individuals on the front lines of their businesses. Each week those with whom the executive has worked are rewarded for what was learned from listening.

One reason for such learning is that these undercover bosses practice *active* listening. They listen for total meaning, respond to the feelings or attitudes underlying the message, and note all communicative cues accompanying the message (facial expressions, body posture, hand movements, eye movements, and breathing). They have learned that listening is an active, dynamic process that requires almost a silent agreement to give total attention when the other person is speaking. They have learned that they cannot be passive; they must actively try to grasp facts and feelings in what they hear. Alertness at every point of the communicative encounter is a prerequisite.

Genuine listening communicates a great deal more than what spoken words can. Leaders who claim they care about what those who follow them think but don't really listen to what they have to say will be judged as insincere and untrustworthy. Leaders who have lasted in industry and in churches practice the art of careful listening that communicates intense and humble curiosity, values the feelings and not simply the knowledge of others, and respects those they lead. When leaders like this listen, people will talk to them and share with them the kinds of information a leader needs to know to make wise decisions that will last for a long time. All of this will have a positive effect on organizational success, health, and climate. And in the end such leaders will be able to pass on a positive legacy.

Reality Check (Q/A)

1. Have you found ways to overcome the 75 percent information loss? Explain.
2. Why is listening effectively so important to build trust?

3. Why do you think people's egos get in the way of them listening to someone else?

4. What are the four interconnecting reasons for why listening is so important and why longtime leaders have come to understand that listening is so significant?

5. Why do you think the heart of listening is the desire to learn?

6. Do you agree with the two key elements that make leaders constructively curious? Why?

7. What have you personally learned about making assumptions when listening to others?

8. How is an assumption a barrier to finding common ground with someone else?

9. Besides the words a speaker presents to you, what are other elements you personally look for? Why?

10. How does anxiety launch a person into a routine of unproductive and destructive behavior?

11. What have you personally discovered about risk when you put your feelings "out there"?

12. How have you learned to communicate respect in your listening behavior?

13. What are three messages of respect that the act of listening sends to a speaker?

14. Do you agree that if leaders wish to have their employees listen to what they say, they must first prove themselves as persons who consistently listen with understanding? Why?

15. How does genuine listening communicate a great deal more than what spoken words can?

Case Study: Listening

Jay Allsop is the youth minister at the Chandler Heights Church. Jay is twenty-seven, and this is his second job as a youth minister. (He was encouraged to leave his first job and find a new church.) He is a talented and responsible individual when he is actively tuned into others.

He enjoys being with people, loves to talk, and always has a story to tell. People generally respond well to him and enjoy being with him when he is attentive to their needs.

Those who have known Jay for a long time typically criticize his shortcomings thusly: He is a poor listener. He is always too busy talking. He seldom pays attention to those around him who are waiting to talk to him about a different subject, one they need help with. Tension is beginning to grow between him and the youth group. The congregational leaders are beginning to notice it as well. They are beginning to sense that some of the problems may be that he is often too busy or preoccupied to listen well. They've also noticed that he does not do well at taking notes. He has been known to forget directions and misunderstand conversations and instructions. In his haste and enthusiasm, he frequently interrupts others when they are busy or when they are talking to him or someone else. So it appears that humility is not his long suit either.

The church leaders are beginning to realize they are facing a prickly situation with Jay. They knew he had been encouraged to leave his previous position, but they were so impressed with the way he interacts with people, and especially young people, that they were willing to overlook any possible hints of past problems. Now they realize they should have investigated more into his background, provided counseling and training about how to be an active listener, and had him practice the new skills he learned.

The chairman of the church leaders has called for a meeting tomorrow night to discuss the situation with Jay. A decision about Jay's future with CHC may have to be made soon.

1. Do you know anyone like Jay? How do you get their attention so they will listen and understand you?
2. If you were either a member of the youth group or a parent invited to the meeting, what would you recommend to them?
3. What role do you think the dismissal from Jay's first job should have on the current case?

4. If you had been an observer in the court of Solomon, as described in 1 Kings 3, what would have been your reactions to and conclusions about the way he handled things?

Notes

[1] Ken Blanchard, *The One Minute Manager* (New York: Morrow, 2003).

[2] Sonya Hamlin, *How to Talk so People Will Listen: Connecting in Today's Workplace* (New York: HarperCollins, 2006), 47.

[3] Douglas Stone, Bruce Patton and Sheila Heen, *Difficult Conversations: How to Discuss What Matters Most* (Penguin, 1999).

[4] Ibid., 46.

[5] John C. Maxwell, *Everyone Communicates, Few Connect: What the Most Effective People Do Differently* (Nashville: Thomas Nelson, 2010), 125.

[6] Albert Ellis, *How to Control Your Anxiety Before it Controls You* (New York: Citadel Press, Kensington Publishing Group, 1998).

[7] Ibid., 209.

Epilogue

A marathon may be the last thing you want to do. Hitting the pavement for twenty-six miles is taxing on the mind as well as the knees. But developing into a long-time Christian leader in your organization or congregation may be exactly what you are training to achieve. Like a marathon runner, longevity in Christian leadership requires enormous preparation, patient determination, and consistent execution of best practices.

Far too often, many people get the privilege to lead others only to be replaced after a few years. Many desire the responsibility, honor and empowerment that come with leading but most discover that leading for a long-time requires more than good intentions and a hunger to stay.

Great achievement takes time. Sure, there are occasions when someone is needed to quickly lead others to a problem's solution and then disappear. But if you feel God wants you to lead others, you probably are not looking to find an opportunity to step in for a moment to then turn around in a few years and relinquish leadership to someone else. Christian leaders, who over time share the trials and overcome the obstacles, are the longtime servants who end up enjoying the successful accomplishment of their church or business's vision.

So do you have what it takes to lead for a long-time? Are you a person others trust and follow through times of adversity and hardships? Does your organization or congregation see you as putting in the effort, focused on a clear direction, and able to motivate others to achieve success?

Groups who want to do something that is truly worthwhile need extraordinary leadership. Our aim has been to share with you what these long-time Christian leaders claim are attributes and actions they have used to excel as leaders within their organization. What they have, you can do.

Some people think leaders are simply born with the skills and capacity to lead. They were born under the right set of circumstances, with the right parents, the best schooling, and all the stars lined up so they could lead. We, however, agree with those who believe the ability to effectively lead can be learned from the wisdom from those who have done it. People have risen to be long-time leaders who at one time were never thought of as becoming a leader.

However, even though long-time leaders can arise from even the most unlikely individuals, leading is not for the faint of heart. It is not for the fearful or the suspicious. It is not for the lazy or self-centered. It is not for those who get easily distracted with the latest quick-fix solutions or who want to go it alone. We believe that leadership longevity for those who trust God with their future requires actions that take time to practice. Christian leaders risk opening themselves to others and welcoming their constructive criticism. They are constantly learning what can help improve what they do and then are willing to share that knowledge with other potential leaders. They are effective communicators who use their skills to authentically listen to others and build community. These traits do not come naturally. They are not genetically wired into some. Long-time leaders are people who are intentional about maturing as leaders, who are trusted and respected.

One of the long-time leaders we interviewed jokingly said, "The secret to being a long-time leader is not dying!" Oh, if that was only true! The reality is that it takes hard work and dedication, and the good news is that it is someone you can do. You may have picked up this book because you are already a leader but wondered what it will take to stay a leader. We want you to know that it is not about being a more charismatic speaker, burnout, or spending your career as a "yes-man".

We hope you will take away from this book the realization that becoming a long-time leader is neither magic nor a secret. It is a combination of several skills, all of which are possible for you to acquire. The long-time leaders we interviewed are like you: individuals trusting God and wanting to make a difference by leading others to do great things for God's kingdom. They worked hard, dreamed big, remained focused, listened, learned, and collaborated with others. Their trust in God and interest in the good of others were bigger than their concern for themselves. They succeed because they knew they were in it for the long haul and were willing to work at it. We know that those who follow their wisdom will find that after many years they too are lifetime leaders.